RECLAIMED

Penny Craswell

RECLAIMED

New homes from old materials

Contents

Left: Rooftop Home has many reclaimed materials, including timber, brass kickplates and fluted terrazzo columns.

Introduction

People have always used materials from their local area to construct buildings – wood from trees, clay from the ground and metals mined from the earth. The practice of repurposing materials from old buildings is almost as old, and now this reuse is more important than ever. Using reclaimed and recycled materials is a vital part of the circular economy that we need to establish if we are going to fight the climate crisis.

Bricks are perfect for reuse – they can be reclaimed, pulled down, cleaned and relaid endlessly. Timber can also be reused again and again, and it hardens with age. Holes can be filled, and timber can be sawn and sanded or left with the beauty of its aged patina. Metal is hard-wearing, making it a good choice for reuse, often without loss of functionality.

As construction methods become more advanced, so has our ability to manufacture new materials from resources we have already extracted from the land. More and more building materials and interior finishes made from recycled waste have been launched to great success. This book explores four key materials: reclaimed brick, timber and metal, and a range of materials reconstituted from waste.

ENVIRONMENTAL ACTION

Why use reclaimed and recycled materials? We are in a climate crisis. We must all do everything we can to fight the environmental degradation of our planet.

This is more than just a problem with rising CO_2 emissions; it is also about pollution and waste. When I was a child, there was an advertising campaign that implored us to 'Do the right thing' and put our rubbish in the bin. Litter was the enemy. Every wrapper, drink container or chip packet featured a picture of a piece of rubbish being put into a bin. I never stopped for a second to wonder where all the rubbish was going. Imagine if the companies producing these products had been responsible for their own waste? How much would it have changed the world? Yet the onus was put firmly on the consumer to throw garbage 'away'.

But, as the German chemist Michael Braungart and American architect William McDonough asked in their 2002 book *Cradle to Cradle: Remaking the Way We Make Things*, where is 'away'? In this groundbreaking book and its 2013 follow up, *The Upcycle: Beyond Sustainability – Designing for Abundance*, they present a radical call to action to rethink how things are made. They propose a shift from a linear cradle-to-grave model of object creation to a circular cradle-to-cradle model.

They also discuss the value of materials and how some processes involve increasing value – upcycling – while some involve lowering the value of the material – downcycling. An example of upcycling is to turn old plastic chopping boards into kitchen benchtops. An example of downcycling is using broken bricks in a gabion wall (a wire structure filled with brick or stone). *Cradle to Cradle* was ahead of its time and incredibly hopeful. It inspired many designers and manufacturers to bring more to the world than they take from it.

But this is very recent history. Not very long ago, design as a discipline felt totally unaligned with sustainability – or any form of ethics, for that matter. It was about style and luxury for the elite. It was aspirational and not concerned with the environment or the other 90 per cent of humanity. Luckily, things have changed, and design is now more closely linked to ethics than ever before, and this includes looking after the environment.

My first book (*Design Lives Here*, 2020) was simple in its premise: to present twenty-one recently designed houses and apartments and highlight one piece of furniture or lighting design. However, one story gave me the inspiration for this book. It was a cat door that interrupted a skirting board, and looked a little like a cartoon mouse hole, designed by architect Sean Humphries of Black Rabbit and made from materials he found in the skip. This spirit of make-do, of using what was already there and diverting materials from landfill was the starting point of this book.

Along the way, I have learned a lot about material use around the world and about sustainability. I discovered that material use is, and should be, local. Not just because so much carbon is wasted on shipping building materials around the world but also because, if you are using materials from construction waste, the available materials will change depending on what is common in your part of the world.

I learned that reusing an existing building (or adaptive reuse) is one of the best ways to avoid construction waste and reduce the amount of raw material extracted from the environment. It also reduces air and water pollution, the amount of land needed for landfill and emissions from landfill sites.

I also discovered how important energy use is in the fight to save the environment. Choosing materials with low embodied energy is important. But improving thermal performance will have an even bigger impact on reducing carbon emissions over the lifetime of the building. The global movement to make buildings more energy efficient with airtight seals and insulation, sometimes called the passive-house movement, is making a significant impact in the reduction of carbon emissions.

But this is not a book about architecture for energy-use reduction, although many of the projects included are extremely energy efficient. This is not a book about reusing existing buildings either, although many of these projects do use existing building stock. And this book is not exhaustive in its exploration of materials used. Instead, it is a presentation of inspirational houses and apartments from around the world with at least one reclaimed material.

The reality is that architects and interior designers can tackle pollution through the choices they make. The construction industry is a huge polluter. Architects have a responsibility to make their buildings long-lasting and to divert useable materials from landfill. Interior designers can do even more – a building might last 100 years or more, but an interior often has a much shorter life.

What's in a name?

Many different terms are used to describe the practice of reusing materials for construction. Some words may mean slightly different things and some have gone in and out of fashion. For example, timber saved from a construction site might be described as 'reclaimed' or 'recycled' timber. When it is reused, it might be described as 'reused' or 'repurposed', or even 'upcycled' or 'downcycled', depending on whether its value goes up or down. It could also be called 'salvaged' although this word carries with it an aesthetic connotation that goes in and out of fashion. However, a new material formed from plastic waste would not be described as 'reclaimed' or 'salvaged', but as 'recycled', 'reconstituted' or 'reformed'.

RECLAIM: To reuse something that has been used before or is considered waste. For example, old timber used as floorboards or bricks that have been taken down, cleaned and reused.

RECYCLE: To reuse something as a whole or to break it down and reform it from component materials. Although 'recycle' usually describes the process of breaking down household waste and reforming it into a new product, it can describe any reuse of an old material.

RECONSTITUTE: To break something down and reform it into a new material. This can be anything from plastic to sawdust to eggshells that has been broken down and remade into something new.

REUSE: To use something that has been used previously. This can be used as an umbrella term that encapsulates the whole category.

SALVAGE: To collect materials considered as waste for reuse.

UPCYCLE: To convert something into something new that has a higher quality or value.

DOWNCYCLE: To convert something into something new that has a lower quality or value.

CIRCULAR ECONOMY: An economy in which materials and resources are circulated to make new products rather than thrown away as waste.

EMBODIED ENERGY: The amount of energy required to make or manufacture a material. The best way to achieve low embodied energy in materials is to reuse them.

OPERATIONAL ENERGY: The amount of energy required for the ongoing operation of a building, including heating and cooling.

THERMAL MASS: The ability of a material to absorb, store and release heat. High thermal mass materials include concrete, brick and stone.

PASSIVE HOUSE: A method of construction that uses airtightness, insulation and double glazing (or triple glazing) to reduce energy consumption.

DESIGN FOR DISASSEMBLY: Construction designed for the eventual removal of materials, for example, using screws instead of glue.

ADAPTIVE REUSE: Reusing an existing building for a new purpose by adapting the design rather than demolishing it and building a new one.

NEW BUILD: A new house or building created from scratch rather than being renovated, extended or otherwise adapted.

SMALL FOOTPRINT: An apartment or a house with a small floor area, which uses less energy and resources than larger builds.

GABION WALL: A wire-framed exterior wall or fence filled with broken bricks, concrete, wood or other scrap materials.

POST-CONSUMER CONTENT: Waste from products used by consumers rather than waste from construction or industry.

Border: Reclaimed bricks at Mole House.

Introduction

PROTOTYPING NEW CONSTRUCTION

In the United Kingdom, architect and academic Duncan Baker-Brown has built a formidable reputation as an expert in architectural building with organic and reused materials. In particular, he recognises the potential of discarded waste as a valuable resource in the future of construction.

Baker-Brown is best known for The House that Kevin Built and The Waste House, both of which are architectural prototypes exploring the use of new materials in construction. The House that Kevin Built (2012) was a prefabricated dwelling made from over 90 per cent organic, replenishable material that was constructed live on television over six days, presented by Kevin McLeod of *Grand Designs*, and then dismantled.

Situated in Brighton and designed and built with the help of students, apprentices and volunteers, The Waste House (2014) took the challenge one step further. Firstly, it was built as a permanent structure. Secondly, it was made not with organic matter, but with waste. Foundations were made from ground-granulated blast-furnace slag supporting a framework of salvaged plywood beams, columns and timber joists. Two thousand used carpet tiles provided weatherproof cladding to the exterior, and the walls were insulated with junk, including 20,000 toothbrushes, 4000 DVD cases, 2000 floppy discs and 2 tonnes of denim offcuts. Overall, 85 per cent of the materials used to build this house were waste from household and construction sites.

Most recently, Baker-Brown has released designs for a new garden pavilion for the Glyndebourne Opera House, made of champagne corks and oyster shells. The pavilion will be both an event space and a teaching and learning place for local community groups. The project is an outstanding example of materials-led creative thinking. The structure will be made of ash trees from the site that have to be cut down due to ash dieback (a disease caused by a fungus, which kills the trees but doesn't adversely affect the timber). Underfired bricks from a local brickworks will be assembled using lime mortar from piles of chalk left over after previous excavations on site. Wall tiles will be manufactured by Local Works Studio from old oyster shells collected on site and from local restaurants. Inside, cork cladding will be made by bio-based materials specialist Biohm by mashing up old corks from wine and champagne bottles into granules and binding them with mycelium – a biodegradable fungal material. Mycelium will also be combined with Gyndebourne's grass clippings and grown to make insulation panels for the building. This design not only uses local and waste materials along the principles of the circular economy, resulting in a low-carbon footprint, it is also designed for disassembly so that it can be reused at the end of the building's life.

This project presents a radical approach to architecture that rethinks every aspect of the design, based on an innovative approach to materials.

Render of Glyndebourne Pavilion interior with cladding made from old champagne corks.

EXPERIMENTAL REUSE

Caroline O'Donnell is an Irish architect and academic who combines architectural research with experimental construction to forge a new path for building with waste. O'Donnell believes that recycling will soon no longer be a choice but a necessity, due to materials scarcity. 'While the sun provides the planet with new energy every day, the materials that we have on the planet are to a large extent finite,' says O'Donnell. 'Soon, it will not so much be important as necessary, as many materials run out in the near future.'

O'Donnell says that reducing the amount of material in landfill is vital. 'In many cases, it is easier and less expensive to rip a building apart and truck it all to landfill sites rather than to carefully take it apart and separate it. We need to build buildings differently so that the scale tips the other way.'

O'Donnell believes that one of the ways to do better is to find materials that are not currently being recycled and transform them into materials that can be recycled, an approach she incorporates into her architectural practice. She is best known for Party Wall, a temporary architectural structure made from the by-product of eco-friendly skateboards. The structure was designed as both shade and seating – 200 removable benches made up the 'wall' of the structure, which could be used as temporary seating for weekday lectures and film screenings. Party Wall was made in a series of community builds called Skateboard Saturdays. Students and associates transformed 3000 pieces of remaindered steel and recycled wood into 150 panels that were used to build the structure.

Although reusing waste is at the heart of O'Donnell's practice, she also says that non-extractive practices are key to the future of architecture. 'When we are using the prefix re-, we are already in trouble,' she says. 'The material has already been produced. Better to start with materials that have not been extractive in their origins.'

Reclaimed

CLEVER MATERIALS

Scientist, engineer and inventor Veena Sahajwalla is researching and developing new materials for construction made from waste. She is the director of the Centre for Sustainable Materials Research and Technology (SM@RT Centre) at the University of New South Wales in Australia. Sahajwalla invented Green Steel using a process she created called polymer injection technology, which offers a cleaner alternative to using coal in steel production.

Sahajwalla is now working on developing new materials from waste, including the production of green ceramics. 'We have to change our mindset and not think of waste as disposable throw-away items,' says Sahajwalla. 'Green ceramics are hybrids that we create from waste glass and textiles, and many other materials. Some of the other products incorporate textile and timber waste. We are continuing to innovate. Thinking about what might look completely impossible today but has to become reality tomorrow.'

What makes the research and development at the SM@RT Centre particularly interesting is the manner of its production. Rather than developing this material through large-scale factories and mass-manufacturing, Sahajwalla and her team have developed micro-factories – small factories of one or more machines that can be installed within the community to convert waste into new materials at a local level. 'These innovative products are very simple,' she says. 'We have this beautiful green ceramic tile that can be manufactured from waste resources, but traditional factories were not doing it.'

As well as creating green ceramics, these micro-factories are also creating plastic filament from waste plastics that can be used as feed stock for 3D printers, making them much more environmentally friendly. Embedding these micro-factories in the community means that locals can transform consumer waste directly into new products, creating jobs in the process. 'No matter where you live, there's enough waste being collected. It's enabling everyone to be part of an economy, which is better for our planet.'

WASTE IS THE NEW BLACK

Author Katie Treggiden has also been researching the use of recycled waste in design. In her book *Wasted: When Trash Becomes Treasure*, she details the work of thirty design studios that are exploring the potential of waste streams to provide the raw materials of the future.

While her research explores furniture and products rather than construction materials, her finger is firmly on the pulse of the transformation of waste into new materials. 'We have an abundance of resources – they're just not in the earth anymore, they are either already in use as something else, polluting the natural environment, or in landfill sites,' says Treggiden. 'The most interesting developments are actually happening at the intersections of different disciplines. Materials made from waste are evolving so quickly that it is often when

a designer collaborates with a chemist or a craftsperson teams up with an engineer that the leaps of imagination we need in this space are happening.'

Treggiden believes that building materials and interior finishes made from waste or 'second-life materials' are becoming more accepted – even sought after. One of the designers featured in her book is Simone Post, who has created a series of rugs made with old sports shoes. Other designers have developed hard surfaces from a range of waste materials that are currently being used as furniture but have the potential to be developed as interior finishes as well. 'This is the decisive decade – we've got less than ten years to address the climate emergency or face a series of irreversible events that could lead to our extinction as a species. There is no silver bullet solution – it's going to take all of us trying and failing and trying again,' says Treggiden.

TAKING RESPONSIBILITY

Being aware of the harm being done to the environment through the extraction of new materials and increasingly large landfill sites should be enough to make us embrace reclaimed materials. But as long as new materials are more affordable, our garbage keeps being taken 'away', and problems such as land being destroyed by landfill sites and plastic building up in the ocean are invisible to us, it is easy to keep buying new.

There are also pitfalls to be aware of when sourcing reclaimed materials. Probably the worst are products that sell a new material with the 'look' of a recycled or salvaged material but without the environmental benefits. Then there are supply chains that exploit people, often in developing countries, by buying materials at a low cost, then selling them for a huge profit. Then there's plain old greenwash – the overstating of environmental benefits. These are issues to be wary of, but they shouldn't put anyone off.

The houses and apartments in this book show the possibilities of reusing old materials and selecting new products made from waste. Each has at least one example, and many have several. The projects are large and small, monochrome and colourful, in big cities, small towns and everywhere in-between, and from many countries around the world, but they all offer ideas and inspiration.

Choosing reclaimed and recycled materials to construct houses and apartments is vital if we are to fight the climate crisis. A bonus is that the result often looks fantastic. Architects and interior designers are in a unique position to influence those around them and make a difference – to use design to inspire people to do the right thing.

Following pages, Left: Reclaimed bricks in muted greys and greens are a key design feature at Kyneton House; Right (inset): Brick screens on the windows at Asper House; Right (border): Reclaimed white bricks create a uniform look at 8-Yard House.

BRICK

12 Mt

12 million tonnes of brick and clay tile debris was generated in the US in 2015.

Office of Resource Conservation and *Recovery, Construction and Demolition Debris Management in the United States*, 2015, US Environmental Protection Agency, 2020.

10 years

In an Australian study, 105 sensors, which took readings every 5 minutes for 10 years, showed that the thermal performance of insulated-cavity brick outperformed cavity brick, brick veneer, reverse brick veneer and lightweight cement-board construction.

Inglis, Cathy, 'Bricks vs the lightweights' in Clarke, Dick (ed), *How to rethink Building Materials: Creating Ecological Housing*, CL Creations, Australia, 2014.

70 Mt

The UK produces 70 million tonnes of masonry and concrete waste per year: 4 per cent is processed to produce secondary aggregate and 29 per cent goes through low-level recycling on or near the site of origin.

Friedman, Avi, *Sustainable Residential Development: Planning and Design for Green Neighbourhoods*, McGraw-Hill, 2008.

Using reclaimed bricks is one of the most straightforward ways of reusing building materials. The availability of recycled bricks depends on how many buildings in the local area are made of brick and how often they are demolished. In parts of the world where residential buildings are mostly made of brick, reused bricks will be easier to find. Double-brick cavity walls with insulation have a high thermal mass, helping to save energy and reduce operational costs. The biggest difficulty is the time and money needed to clean them, especially in countries with high labour costs.

This section includes houses made from reclaimed bricks bought from seconds' suppliers and one house made from bricks that have been reclaimed on site. Used externally, internally or both, the bricks in these houses are consistent in colour, mixed up to create a patchwork effect or painted for a uniform look. The benefits of using reclaimed bricks include the embodied energy saved in not firing new bricks, the diversion of waste from landfill, and their inherent beauty.

Left: White bricks with white-flowering plants at 8-Yard House.
Centre: Reclaimed bricks with a custom textured mortar in the interior of Kyneton House.
Right: Interiors with reclaimed bricks at House V.

8-Yard House

LOCATION	Melbourne, Australia
ARCHITECT	Studio Bright
REUSED MATERIAL	Bricks

Architecture office Studio Bright used reclaimed bricks, lightly bagged and painted cream, to create a sense of history at 8-Yard House, a new build in suburban Melbourne. 'I like it that non-architects are not sure if it's a new or an old house,' says architect Melissa Bright. 'Maybe that's connected to the material choices we made.'

Situated on a street full of single-fronted Victorian houses, the house previously on this site was poorly built, with a number of badly handled additions, and could not be adapted. The challenge for the architects was to create a new house in an old street that still felt like it was part of the neighbourhood.

The first step was to organise the volume on the large site. One priority was to catch northern sunlight, another was to not overshadow the neighbours. Rather than separating the site into only two zones – a house at the front and garden at the back – the outdoor spaces were divided into a series of courtyards and gardens that were distributed along the length of the site.

In all, there are eight outdoor spaces, or yards, of different sizes, which gives rise to the name of the house. The owners wanted a pool, but if it had been put in the backyard it would become the focal point, and more space would be taken up with pool fencing. Instead, the pool was brought forward, and it stretches along the northern side of the house.

At the front of the house, a perforated brick wall screens a small outdoor courtyard created outside the main bedroom on the northern side. Another small courtyard was created further back, towards the middle of the house, on the southern border. At the back, a partially paved garden is bookended with another structure – a two-storey studio and garage – that faces the back alley.

Reclaimed brick is an important part of the design. The front facade has a skin of solid brick on the first storey above the ground floor, which is clad in grey timber. At the top of the facade, a circular form in brick protrudes above the roofline, echoing the semicircular shape of the ornate Victorian plaster facade of the house next door. On the northern side of the facade, the brick forms a perforated screen that conceals the small front courtyard off the main bedroom.

Inside the house, reclaimed bricks are used as interior finishes alongside timber in the living room and kitchen. The kitchen island is made with brick, with curved brickwork forming recesses for knees under the stone bench. Outside, the brickwork is omnipresent. The pool and the green courtyard gardens are all set against a backdrop of cream brick. In the outdoor spaces leading from the pool to the back garden, a series of outdoor courtyards is separated by brick beams that create a material connection above head height between the exterior brick walls and the house itself.

At the front of the house is an intimate living area lined in dark timbers and brick. It looks almost like a library or an old-fashioned sitting room. 'In some ways this is our new

Above: Reclaimed white bricks from the facade form a balustrade around the rooftop garden.
Right: Front facade in white reclaimed brick with grey-painted timber.

"old" house part,' says Bright. The front bedroom is the same, and floor-to-ceiling curtains create a sense of cosiness and dark cocooning.

After this section, the house really opens out. A sense of connection is achieved by the distribution of space and connection to the outdoors. The kitchen space is separated from the side garden by glass, then a couple of steps lead down into a sunken living space with views to the garden on two sides.

Upstairs, the kids' bedrooms are set out in a row. Desks are built into the corridor to draw the kids out of their bedrooms so that, while they are doing homework or on their computers, they are sitting side by side in a more social space. A large rumpus room with a TV on this floor opens to the rooftop garden, again encouraging socialising and providing a connection to the outdoors.

8-Yard House shows that, even with a new build, a sense of history can be created through the intelligent use of materials. This house could easily have been built with new brick, but it would have had a totally different feel – one that was more monolithic and less rich. The selection of reclaimed brick has given this house a coherence that meshes perfectly with the focus on nature of the eight outdoor yards, and the cream paint contrasts wonderfully with the green planting throughout.

8-Yard House

The front living room has rich, dark interiors with an old
wood-burning stove.

View from the garden to the sunken living room, with reclaimed
brick inside and out.

Left: One of the smaller 'yards' is a courtyard off the dining room.
Above: View through to the kitchen, with windows bringing in daylight.

Top left: Curved brick recesses for knees in the kitchen.
Bottom left: Desks upstairs for the children.

Top right: Corridor with views of the garden.
Bottom right: White bathroom tiles are laid vertically.

The sunken living room is surrounded by greenery, with gardens
on the side and to the back.

The front master bedroom opens onto a small garden with
a perforated screen wall that forms part of the facade.

Built-in seating upstairs has views of the roof garden
and nearby rooftops.

RECLAIMED: BRICKS

The bricks from the demolished house were sold, but instead of buying brand-new bricks the architects chose to work with reclaimed bricks. This decision wasn't just based on the aesthetic qualities of the reclaimed bricks, although their colouring is an important part of what makes this house so appealing. It was also a conscious choice to create a sense of history for this new building.

'We're so used to working with old houses that when we work with a new house we can't help but make it feel old,' explains Bright. 'Recycled bricks have got a history and a layer to them that you can't necessarily get in a new material.'

The bricks were found by Tim Faughlin from Bayview Brick and Block Laying. They are variegated and some have stamps indicating where they were made. About 30 bricks have a Melbourne Olympics stamp that features the Olympic rings and the words 'Glen Iris 1956'. There was a huge variation of colours, including cream, red, yellow and white, and some bricks had dark patches, but they were all bagged and given a light paint to create a cream finish, which gave them a more even look.

'Bagging them is not really normal, but when you are working with architects there's nothing really normal,' says Faughlin. 'They were difficult to lay. You can't be quick with them; you have to be slow because of the different sizes and faces. But it was enjoyable.'

ARCHITECT	Studio Bright
PROJECT TEAM	Melissa Bright, Robert McIntyre, Todd de Hoog, Maia Close, Emily Watson, Pei She Lee
BUILDER	Basis Builders
ENGINEER	Meyer Consulting
LANDSCAPE	Peachy Green
BRICKLAYER	Bayview Brick & Block
PHOTOGRAPHY	Rory Gardiner

Above: The house reveals itself in layers of reclaimed brick.
Right: The pool has been placed at the side so it doesn't dominate the rear garden.

Brick House

LOCATION	Vancouver, Canada
ARCHITECT	Campos Studio
REUSED MATERIAL	Bricks

Brick is not the standard material for residential buildings in Vancouver. While there are a number of old brick buildings in the centre of town, new houses are almost always made of timber. Brick House by Campos Studio is remarkable for being made of reclaimed brick – a responsible selection and one that has a great effect on its aesthetic.

Early in the design stage, the architects decided that rather than going with a brick box with holes for doors and windows, they would create openings at the corners of the house, relieving the heaviness of the brick with glass and bringing light into the house, while providing views of the outside. 'There's no perforations, no holes in the brick walls with a lintel. Instead, it's an exercise in carving out corners,' says Javier Campos.

Designed over three storeys, the layout of the house was largely determined by the make-up of the family: a couple with four active children under the age of 12. The architectural response was one of flexibility – every space had to be both useful and a site for play. The interiors feature light blonde timbers and minimal colours, and bespoke in-built milled cabinetry offers storage. The cabinets often perform two functions. 'Almost everything has two different uses,' explains senior designer Czarina Ray. 'It's a guard to the staircase and also a desk. Or a guard to the void to the basement, but also a minibar where they hide their party drinks.'

On the ground floor, the front of the house includes a small, simply furnished dining room with views of the front garden. The kitchen is in the centre of the ground-floor space and has cabinetry on one side and an island with a slim-profile marble top. A large in-built furniture storage unit in white and light blonde timber separates the kitchen from the staircase and can be used to hide items in cupboards or display them on shelving. At the back of the ground floor, the sunken main living room is accessed by two stairs at the side, and a ledge to the kitchen provides a backrest for an in-built sofa in sumptuous caramel-brown leather.

The staircases down to the basement and up to the top floor align with each other, and each stair is accompanied by millwork cabinetry to form the stair core. Upstairs is the main bedroom with ensuite, and two rooms for the girls that each have their own bathroom. At the top of the stairs is a small vestibule with bench seating along the windows that look out to a rooftop terrace. The built-in storage next to the staircase on this level forms a desk and there is more storage at the top of the stairs. This creates a number of ways to use a space that could easily have just been a thoroughfare. Other details stand out – a pegboard in milled timber, and the simple beauty of the bathrooms with their timber cabinetry and elegant flooring of yellow diamond-shaped tiles. Downstairs is a large playroom, the two boys' rooms and their shared bathroom, the laundry and storage.

Above: The vertical glass window in the sunken living room lightens the heaviness of the brick structure.
Right: At the back of the house, the colour variation in the reclaimed brick adds history.

As well as the internal staircase, there are external stairs leading from the ground floor down to a basement-level entry. This is how the family enter into the house – they can drop everything at this entrance and store their coats, umbrellas and more. This external staircase also connects the outdoors to the basement, bringing light into this level.

The idea of play was vital in the design of this house. The architects were inspired by Isamu Noguchi's playground designs that created 'noncommittal structures' – architectural forms designed to stimulate children's imaginations. 'Lots of times, kids come up with new interactions and ways to explore,' explains Ray. 'We saw them playing with things or creating games we never expected.' This house is full of opportunities for play, like a place to jump from the kitchen to the couch, or a freestanding column to swing around on, or cupboards to climb in and under. 'Everything has this transformative potential brought about by kids wanting to play,' says Campos.

Campos Studio has been practising sustainable architecture since it began. Their first project was an off-the-grid house in Mexico and their early work was all about efficient energy use and bringing design to the passive-house movement. 'In the early 2000s, passive houses looked like they were designed by engineers,' says Campos. Energy efficiency has been a huge focus for the sustainability movement in North America. Another focus has been on smaller living options, and the tiny house movement has made a big difference in creating environmentally friendly housing. The recognition of the importance of reclaimed materials in sustainable housing is also underway. Projects like Brick House show just how beautiful reclaimed materials can be.

Brick

Left: Large windows in the dining room bring the outdoors in.
Above: Bricks in the dining room interior have been painted white.

The living room has been lowered to follow the slope of the site.

The interiors are minimal but have the potential to be turned
into sites for play.

Brick House

Top left: White and timber joinery.
Bottom left: Timber pegboard in a bedroom.

Top right: The kitchen cupboards back onto the stairs.
Bottom right: A skylight brings light into the bathroom.

The built-in furniture at the top of the staircase forms a desk
and storage unit.

The kitchen is the hub of the house and exhibits a playful
approach to cabinetry.

Brick House

Openings at the corners of the house relieve the heaviness
of the brick.

RECLAIMED: BRICKS

This house has made the most of its reclaimed bricks by leaving them unrendered. 'The client initially wanted a white house with black windows, but we wanted to show the recycled brick,' explains Javier Campos. 'We made a deal with them that they would wait for six months and, if they still wanted to change it then, we would paint it white. But in the end, they loved the recycled brick look.' The bricks were sourced from several different places and were mixed up to create a random pattern of colours – red with pink, blue, white and yellow variations. 'The history of the different remnants of the buildings can be seen in the recycled brick,' says Ray. 'It adds texture and interest to the final building.'

ARCHITECT	Campos Studio
PROJECT TEAM	Javier Campos, Alix Demontrond, Czarina Ray
BUILDER	Overton Construction
ENGINEER	Equilibrium
PHOTOGRAPHY	Ema Peter

Above: The reclaimed bricks come from demolished buildings in the old, central part of the city.

Asper House

LOCATION	Asper, Belgium
ARCHITECT	Kaderstudio
REUSED MATERIAL	Bricks

Reclaimed bricks were an important ingredient in the design of Asper House by Kaderstudio. When architects Stijn Elsen and Simone Valerio were approached to design a house in a rural part of East Flanders in Belgium, they wanted to preserve the rural essence of the area through an agricultural architecture typology that uses the historic material of choice – brick.

The owners had received this plot of land from their parents – a common practice in this part of the world – and the land had only recently been parcelled into four and was still in use for growing corn when the architects first visited the site. 'At first we weren't sure whether we should take on the project at all, as we didn't want to contribute to the conversion of farmland into urban sprawl,' says Elsen.

The solution the architects came up with was to create a family house that looked like an agricultural building and could even be used that way in the future. 'We tried to develop the project in the most sustainable way we could think of. Looking at typology, we designed it as a barn,' says Valerio.

The outer envelope of the building is a timeless form – a two-storey brick shell with six concrete columns that support a pitched roof. A second layer was built inside the shell. This wooden structure is completely independent and can be removed without affecting the brick or the roof. 'Eventually, the idea is to use it for storing agricultural machines or weed or other agricultural stuff,' says Elsen.

The normal building process was reversed. Rather than building a structure in wood and decorating it with brick, the building was made in structural brick, with timber built inside the frame. The concrete slab and concrete stairs add to the thermal mass of the building.

Another important aspect of the design was to rotate the building 90 degrees so that the long facade of the house is not parallel to the street but perpendicular. This disrupts the more usual placement, which obscures the land and makes the street look like any other village. Rotating the house makes the land adjacent to it visible from the street and adds a sense of nature to the streetscape – the architects refer to this as 'Flemish imagery'. This positioning also means that the house can enter a dialogue with adjacent farm buildings, creating a relationship that is flexible and has a sense of belonging without being generic. On the western elevation, a timber facade allows for a generous porch on the concrete slab, creating an inside–outside space that feels like part of the house.

Inside, large windows create a connection to the outdoors and the absence of fences between this property and the adjacent corn fields make this home feel like a rural idyll. The open-plan rooms on the ground floor are generous. Apart from the staircase and a space for bicycles, the rest of this floor is one large room with a kitchen at one end, dining in the centre and living space at the far end. The window at the northern end of the house (which gets the least light in the Northern

Above: The house is supported by a two-storey brick shell and six concrete columns.
Right: The brick exterior is punctuated to create a screen for the window in the living room.

Hemisphere winter) has an external brick screen, called a claustra. Upstairs, the staircase separates the master bedrooms and ensuite from the other bedrooms and family bathroom, and there is a study at the far end of the floor.

In creating Asper House, the architects have interrogated the typical buildings in this rural part of East Flanders, which contribute to urban sprawl in this part of Europe. By rethinking the construction method, materials and even the orientation of the building, they have created a hybrid that combines a farm-style typology with a new concept for family living. This house celebrates the land and its history, rather than replacing it. Even the way they have photographed the house in two stages, first as a basic concrete slab, structure and reclaimed brick walls to show how this building could be repurposed as an agricultural building, then as a finished residential house with interiors, shows the thoughtfulness of this approach to architecture. It is an approach that combines the best of history and tradition with a new way of thinking about residential architecture.

Asper House

One side of the building is clad in untreated wood built inside
the brick shell.

Brick

The house is perpendicular to the road, so more of the landscape
is visible to passers-by.

Left: The view from the kitchen is of agricultural land.
Above: The long space on the ground floor functions as kitchen, dining and living room.

The living room has a concrete slab floor and doors that open
directly onto the porch.

RECLAIMED: BRICKS

The selection of local, reclaimed bricks for the exterior shell of the house illustrates Kaderstudio's sustainable approach to architecture, which focuses on circular design – materials are not discarded or recycled, but reused. Bricks are an excellent example, as they can be used again and again. The only requirement is the labour of cleaning the bricks and the energy used to transport them, and this can be reduced if local bricks are used.

Bricks are plentiful in Belgium because they are a common building material for residential and farm buildings. There is a famous saying – 'Every Belgian is born with a brick in their stomach' – referencing the national aspiration of home ownership.

Reclaimed bricks are also a perfect fit for Kaderstudio's architectural style, which is simple, slow and low-tech. The architects visited six or seven different brick dealers in barns see how the bricks were cleaned, how they worked together visually, and their size, which had to meet precise dimensions. 'For Asper, we wanted a brick that was very simple and pure, but which also had dimensions that were strict,' says Elsen.

ARCHITECT	Kaderstudio
PROJECT TEAM	Stijn Elsen, Simone Valerio Andrea Lusquiños Mansilla
ENGINEER	Util Struktuurstudies
PHOTOGRAPHY	Kaderstudio

Above: The bricks vary in colour but were chosen for their precise dimensions to get an even finish.

The pitched roof extends past the edge of the porch.

Mole House

LOCATION	Hackney, UK
ARCHITECT	Adjaye Associates
REUSED MATERIAL	Brick, timber floorboards, front gate, masonry and concrete

Mole House has a long and complicated history. It is famous for being owned by the 'mole man', William Lyttle. Lyttle was a British civil engineer who owned the house from the 1960s until he was evicted in 2006. The urban myth is that he began an excavation for a new wine cellar and ended up creating a radiating network of caverns and tunnels that were up to 8 metres deep and 20 metres long.

The truth is a little less dramatic. Lyttle only dug about 1.5 metres down, partly undermining the neighbour's foundations to the west and pavements to the east and west. Lyttle was also a hoarder. When his neighbours expressed concern, the council seized the property and removed 33 tonnes of waste, including three cars and a boat. They plugged the tunnels with 2000 tonnes of aerated concrete and built a fence around the house. Mole House remained derelict and abandoned, even after Lyttle's death in 2010.

It makes sense that this ruinous house was bought by an artist who works with junk. Sue Webster fell in love with the building after passing it on the street. After much negotiating, she bought the house from Lyttle's estate in 2012 and hired Ghanaian–British architect David Adjaye to do the redesign.

It would have been cheaper to knock Mole House down, but Webster was keen to preserve its layers of history, including the dilapidated original building and Lyttle's additions and alterations. 'What I love about working with Sue on this project is that for her, even though she is living there, the home is really a statement about art. The idea of making a work is as important as living there,' says Adjaye.

The design process was lengthy. First, the internal structure was gutted, and sections of the house were mapped to preserve the plaster of the original structure. Much of the council's aerated concrete, as well as areas of earth and original building materials, was removed to expand the basement, which is now a huge open-plan living space. 'The design is born from an archaeological exercise, a gradual reveal of time through the process of excavation – an unearthing of up to 2000 tonnes of filler concrete revealing several years of fossilised domestic history,' says Adjaye. Multiple entrances to this new basement level follow the same path as Lyttle's tunnels. Living spaces open onto a sunken landscaped garden, and two entrances are directly accessible from the driveway and the road.

Inside, a large cross-shaped concrete structure in the centre of the plan divides each floor into four zones, supporting new floor slabs and bracing external walls. Original internal walls and floors – many of which were beyond repair – were removed completely. An existing wall that previously divided the house was removed, creating expansive rooms lined in exposed concrete and timber, both reclaimed and new. Natural light floods in through full-height windows and doors on each storey and a skylight on the top floor.

The front door leads to an open-plan living space that has a circular dining table and chairs to one side and a simple wooden kitchen at the far end. The Douglas fir plywood used for the kitchen, staircase, bookshelf and wardrobes is the same plywood that was used to cast the concrete structure – another example of reuse. In the middle of the space is a relaxed living zone with wooden bookshelves along one wall, a low navy sofa and a sculptural Max Lamb coffee table. Webster's artworks are placed throughout the house, from her punk leather jackets to a monumental work tracing her whole life history, installed like a crime scene on the two-storey wall of her downstairs artist's studio.

The owner's irreverent sense of humour and love of punk is apparent everywhere. There are two bedrooms upstairs – the main bedroom and another that is furnished with a bed and a leather punching bag that hangs from a ceiling hook. The upstairs bathroom has black-and-white zigzag tiles, and the heated towel rails have Webster's first name, SUE, pressed into the copper pipes.

Downstairs, Webster's studio is huge, with in-built furniture that forms an office, and a sink for washing brushes. This room leads directly to the sunken garden through bay windows with patinated bronze frames. A concrete slab the size of a doormat on the threshold features the words 'Fucking Beautiful'.

The exteriors are a mix of old and new. The owner's interest in preserving Mole House's history can be seen in the original entry, where a beaten-up green gate at the front corner of the property has been retained, as have the building's facades above ground level, complete with crumbling stucco and peeling paint. In contrast, a new single horizontal slate sheet replaces the original gable-end pitched roof, and the front windows have a mirrored vinyl finish on them for privacy, almost like a pair of reflective sunglasses.

Mole House had an ethos of recycling and make-do long before its modern redesign. When he was tunnelling, Lyttle kept the building from falling by using handmade concrete pillars that were strengthened with pipes, junk metal and waste that he had collected and recycled for this purpose. Remnants of these pillars can be seen in the garden, contrasting with the aerated concrete from the council's attempt to plug the mole man's tunnels, and the rational and precise concrete that Adjaye has added.

Adjaye and his team believe that architecture as a process is fundamentally abusive – both of the planet and of human rights – but they are attempting to amend that by prioritising smarter, responsive and more ecologically sound materials. With Mole House, Adjaye has created a dialogue between old and new materials. The decision to retain and preserve, while also adding function and a new aesthetic layer, is part of this design's success.

Right: Concrete was used like a horizontal band to support the house, creating a new basement level.

On the top landing, the balustrade to the plywood timber staircase
doubles as the back of a built-in desk.

The dining room at the front of the house, with views of the road.

Above: The living room has a palette of exposed concrete and reclaimed timber.
Right: A huge artist's studio on the basement level has openings in the same position as the original tunnels.

Mole House

Wooden floorboards are reclaimed pine, while one-way glass
windows are mirrored outside for privacy.

The Douglas fir plywood that forms the staircase was first used
to cast the concrete structure.

Reclaimed bricks purchased for the project were carefully matched
to the existing bricks.

RECLAIMED: BRICKS

Thanks to the property's unusual history, the renovation and extension of Mole House was an especially complex design challenge for the architects, and this includes its story of reuse. Around 15,000 reclaimed bricks were used in the project to shore up foundations where there was excess damage, and to create a brick wall surrounding the house and gardens. These bricks, with an earthy palette of reds and browns, and yellows, blacks and whites, were sourced from demolished walls within the house and reclamation suppliers.

Care was taken to match the reclaimed bricks to the existing bricks of the original house. The bricks were laid using a mix of lime, white cement and builder's sand, and washed with a diluted concrete pigment to age them. This inclusion reflects Adjaye's approach to materials within the Mole House project more generally: 'Designed with its domestic history in mind, the reinstated building creates an architecture that acknowledges notions of recycling both historically and within materiality.'

ARCHITECT	Adjaye Associates
PROJECT TEAM	David Adjaye, Yohannes Bereket
ELECTRICAL ENGINEER	Parry Page
GENERAL CONTRACTOR	Parry Page
LANDSCAPE ARCHITECT	Adjaye Associates
MECHANICAL/PLUMBING ENGINEER	Parry Page
STRUCTURAL ENGINEER	Alcock Lees Partnership Ltd
PHOTOGRAPHY	Ed Reeve

Above: The wall of the front facade was deliberately left untouched to show the history of the house.

Kyneton House

LOCATION	Kyneton, Australia
ARCHITECT	Edition Office
REUSED MATERIAL	Bricks

Above: The house was centred on the site to provide garden views on all sides.
Right: Reclaimed brick walls are interrupted by floor-to-ceiling glazed windows and doors.

Located in the town of Kyneton, 90 kilometres north-west of Melbourne, Australia, this house makes use of a limited selection of materials, including reclaimed brick. The site originally had a red-brick house on it, but it had fallen into a state of disrepair and was demolished to make way for this new build. Although the architects considered reusing the red bricks from the original house, it was more cost-effective to sell them and buy reclaimed bricks. This also allowed the architects from Edition Office to choose a more muted colour that ties in with the landscape and the historic buildings in the town.

The owners are a retired couple who were downsizing from a larger rural house to this simple, single-storey home. Keen gardeners, they planned to transplant much of their old garden onto the new site. The architects centred the house on the site to make the garden accessible and visible from each room. Setting the house back from the street also meant that gardening in the front yard could be a social activity, making it easy for the owners to meet their new neighbours.

The design of Kyneton House is characterised by a repeated gesture of thickened brick walls surrounding a recess that, when viewed from above, looks like a square bracket or long U-shape. The walls are broken up with glazed windows and doors, creating a rhythm unlike the usual uniform brick skin of a building. The U-shape presents to the exterior as a thickened wall or protective shell. Inside the house it forms a recess – a floor-to-ceiling niche that provides a space for nesting in-built furniture. In the kitchen, this niche is filled in with cabinetry and the kitchen sink, and in the living room and the bedrooms it is furnished with a simple wooden shelf. Where these niches appear, the walls are up to 300 mm thick, with insulation between two brick layers. 'This figurative gesture – we call them cups or niches, but the architectural language would be *pochés* – creates a really clear rhythm and consistency for the house,' says architect Kim Bridgland.

Other than these brick niches, the plan of the house is simple. The entry corridor opens on the right to an open-plan kitchen, dining and living room and on the left to a corridor from which the other rooms are accessed. Everything is on the ground floor, and the halls and doorways are wide enough for wheelchair access, making this a perfect house for planning into old age. In each room, the lofted ceilings follow the form of the roof, creating angled ceilings that soar to almost 6 metres at their pinnacle. 'Light, when it comes up, billows around and gives a particular sense of space,' says Bridgland.

The material selections are also simple. As well as reclaimed brick, there is a pale, low-carbon, burnished concrete floor that functions as the slab of the house and is hydronically heated. Sustainably sourced Australian blackbutt timber is used in the kitchen, joinery and door and window frames. The roof is galvanised steel, and the ceilings are a cost-effective ceiling board – these are the only materials that differ internally and externally. The reclaimed brick, sustainable timber and glazing are the same inside and out. 'As we go in, the material language is the same, with the exception of the white ceiling,' says Bridgland. 'The house isn't yelling "Look at me" – it's framing the space that can be occupied.'

Sustainable features of the house include an energy system that is powered by solar panels – no gas or fossil fuels are needed. All heating is through an air-exchange heat pump and natural cooling comes from the building's thermal mass, solar orientation and air circulation. 'The house needed to meet the owners' high sustainable agenda and the pursuit of a low-carbon footprint. There's the aesthetic concern and then there's that technical or social ambition,' says Bridgland.

For what feels like a spacious house that drinks in its landscape, Kyneton House has a restrained footprint. And although timber, concrete and steel are celebrated, the hero really is the bricks. The unusual thickening of walls brings a sense of monumentality and unique character to the house. That this has been achieved with reclaimed bricks, bringing a sense of history and place, and keeping these hardworking materials out of landfill, just makes this design more impressive.

Inside, reclaimed brick is one of the dominant materials,
along with timber.

Left: The kitchen has simple lines thanks to joinery that reaches from the floor to the ceiling.

Above: The kitchen combines natural timber with black stone, taps and sinks.

Above: This brick niche, which looks like a long U-shape or *poché*
from above, is repeated throughout the plan.
Right: Neutral colours give a uniform look in the bathroom.

Top left: Dining room niche with timber shelf.
Bottom left: Wide front door.

Top right: Everything is generously proportioned.
Bottom right: Reclaimed bricks are grey with tinges of green.

In the bedroom, the wooden shelf in the niche forms a simple desktop.

A lower bench in the living room niche provides space
for plants and seating.

RECLAIMED: BRICKS

Reclaimed bricks in a soft muted colour are an important characteristic of this house, both visually and in its construction. The reclaimed bricks brought in for this new build reflect both the green and grey hues of the landscape, and the green and grey bricks of the historic buildings in Kyneton's town centre. The selected bricks are the cheapest grade of recycled bricks and have a custom mortar finish that is dry rubbed over the bricks, covering up imperfections without losing any character. 'Reclaimed bricks have a character that is difficult to acquire with a new brick,' says Bridgland. 'The idea of reclaimed is fantastic and it goes far beyond an aesthetic concern. From a circular economy perspective, these are carbon value assets that mature over time.'

ARCHITECT	Edition Office
PROJECT TEAM	Kim Bridgland, Aaron Roberts, Erin Watson
BUILDER	Dettmann Homes
PHOTOGRAPHY	Ben Hosking

Above: The architects tested several mortar finishes before selecting this textured finish for the bricks.

House V

LOCATION	Bratislava, Slovakia
ARCHITECT	Martin Skoček
REUSED MATERIAL	Bricks

Lining the inside of your home with recycled bricks isn't just an intelligent way to reuse construction waste when pulling down a house and putting up a new one, it also creates a unified and beautiful interior finish. That's certainly the case for House V, a new building designed by Martin Skoček in the small borough of Vajnory in Bratislava, Slovakia. The owners originally approached Skoček to build an extension onto the existing house, but the condition of the house was too poor, and the structure was deemed irreparable. Instead, the house was demolished to make way for a new structure.

The brief was for a three-bedroom, two-bathroom house suitable for a young family and the architectural response is simple – a linear plan with a gabled titanium-zinc roof. The shape of the building is inspired by the agricultural buildings in this part of rural Bratislava. The living space, bedrooms and bathrooms are all on the same level. The house runs along the northern border of the site, with bedrooms at the front and back of the property. The entry is at the side of the house and opens straight onto the living room in the centre of the house. The main living, dining and kitchen space, with its soaring ceilings, is connected by sliding glass doors directly to the garden that runs along the side of the house. 'The plan arrangement is inspired by a three-part Slovak house where the central space becomes the so-called *pitvor*,' explains Skoček. '[The] front hall of the house [is] oriented onto the garden, which is its inseparable part.'

Like the form and plan of the house, the materiality is also extremely simple. But unlike houses that have rendered and painted interior walls and exterior walls of exposed brick, House V's exteriors are a light-grey rendered masonry, and the interiors are raw brick. The bricks have a history of reuse and wear that add character to the space, meaning that furnishings can remain simple for a dramatic look.

The ceilings are pitched and lined with timbers, many of which are also reclaimed. Discussing the shape of the roof, Skoček says, 'A significant structural element is the shaping of the roof truss, allowing in eastern light though skylights and thus respecting the continuous roof massing visible from the garden.'

In the main room, where reclaimed bricks are the hero, the pitched ceilings are high, bringing a sense of monumentality to the space, and the windows offer views of greenery in the garden. The kitchen is formed by a long stainless-steel island bench with a sink and a bank of timber cabinets behind it. Tucked behind the cabinets are a bathroom, toilet and wardrobe built into a timber 'box' – an architectural insertion into the space that does not touch the walls or ceiling. At the front of the house is the master bedroom and ensuite, and at the back there are two bedrooms, one with a bed accessed by a ladder above a desk. There is also a children's swing hanging from the bed construction.

Above: The entrance to the house is on the side, accessed by a path through the gardens.
Right: The exterior is contemporary in white with grey and black metal.

Where the house is split into smaller rooms, the angled shape of the ceiling trusses has been lowered, rather than opting for a horizontal ceiling form, creating interesting geometries. In the main bedroom ensuite, a freestanding bath has been placed in the centre, below the apex of the pitched ceiling, with clerestory windows bringing in light. Behind the bed in the main bedroom, new timber has been used for cupboards and a large bedhead, and a deep aluminium-framed window provides views of the garden.

This house is remarkable for its material simplicity. The pitched roof and wooden ceiling, the internal bricks, the connection to the garden all create a harmonious sense of proportion for the whole, and thoughtful details play within.

House V

The main living space opens directly onto the garden, with dining
tables inside and out.

The pool and garden are bordered by the neighbours' external brick walls.

Bricks from the old house were used to line the interiors.

House V

Top left: Bath under a clerestory window.
Bottom left: Study window.

Top right: View of the house from the rear.
Bottom right: Glazed corridor.

An oversized square window offers a magnificent view of the garden.

The bed above the study is accessed via a ladder, with a net for safety.

RECLAIMED: BRICKS

What could be simpler than demolishing a brick house, brick by brick, saving those bricks, cleaning them and then using them to build a new house? In other parts of the world, it is cheaper to sell bricks from a demolished house and buy new reclaimed bricks, but in Slovakia reusing the bricks on site is the cheaper option. Skoček says it was 'both an economic and an ecological decision'. This solution also has the added benefit of retaining the same brick colouring as other rural houses and farms in this part of Bratislava, but moves them inside to provide a fresh new aesthetic. Sometimes reusing the same materials in a different space can be enough to make it look like a completely contemporary redesign.

ARCHITECT	Martin Skoček
PROJECT TEAM	Martin Skoček, Lucia Miklová
LANDSCAPE ARCHITECT	LABAK
PHOTOGRAPHY	Matej Hakar

Above: Ample glazing with interiors that combine brick, concrete and timber.

Following pages, Left: Most of the timber used at Hachi Lily House is from demolished buildings.
Right (inset): The timber window frames at Smash Repair House are all reclaimed.
Right (border): Vertical tiles filter light at Ruang Tekuni.

TIMBER

10%

The Australian Government estimates that around 10 per cent of timber products imported and sold into Australia comes from illegal operations, but it could be much higher.

Inglis, Cathy, 'Bricks vs the lightweights' in Clarke, Dick (ed), *How to Rethink Building Materials: Creating Ecological Housing*, CL Creations, 2014.

8 Mt

Around 8 million tonnes of wood is thrown out in the UK every year, yet 80 per cent is reusable. The UK's Wood Recycling Network diverted 8500 tonnes of wood from the waste stream in 2012.

Fletcher, Cat, 'What a waste' in Baker-Brown, Duncan, *The Re-Use Atlas: A Designer's Guide Towards the Circular Economy*, Routledge, 2017.

30%

In the US, wood waste is the second-largest component of construction and demolition debris after concrete. It makes up 20 to 30 per cent of total building-related debris.

LeBlanc, Rick, 'The importance of wood recycling in C&D management', *The Balance Small Business*, 26 November 2018, <thebalancesmb.com/wood-recycling-construction-2877760>.

Reclaimed timber has many benefits and few drawbacks. It can be extremely beautiful, thanks to a patina that accumulates with time and wear. It is also an attractive option because of the increasing difficulty of sourcing high-quality new timbers, particularly hardwood, which comes from old-growth forests.

Reusing timber is a common practice across the world. This section includes projects from Australia, Asia, Europe and North America. The types of timber vary according to local construction methods and the history of timber production.

Most reclaimed timber is sourced from construction sites. Joinery, windows and doors can be restored and reused, and larger pieces of timber can be sourced from industrial buildings, old warehouses and rural sheds. Reclaimed timber can last hundreds of years and becomes harder as it ages. Paint or nails can be removed, holes filled and pieces cut down to size. It can also be sanded for a smooth finish or left untouched to retain its patina.

Left: Reclaimed timber lines an arch at MD Apartment.
Centre: Dark aged teak is reclaimed at MD Apartment.
Right: Stair detail at Smash Repair House.

Smash Repair House

LOCATION	Sydney, Australia
ARCHITECT	Matt Elkan Architect
REUSED MATERIAL	Timber door and window frames, timber for tables, bricks

Timber is the unifying material in the interiors of Smash Repair House, a home in the inner-Sydney suburb of Paddington designed by Matt Elkan Architect. Reclaimed timber was used for the doors and windows in the house, and there are a lot of them. Despite the property being bounded by brick walls on all sides, there are doors and windows on both storeys that look onto an interior courtyard, plus openings to an outdoor room created on the first floor. Bricks from demolished walls were also reused in the creation of a third storey, and reclaimed timber was used to make two new tables.

The renovation and extension of this home is also an exercise in adaptive reuse. It was previously a two-storey smash repair shop for cars, dating back to the 1960s. Elkan's design now forms a U-shape around an internal courtyard on both storeys as well as a new mezzanine third level. The main living, dining and kitchen spaces are on the first floor, which also has an outdoor deck that is connected to the kitchen with sliding doors. On this floor there is also a bedroom and bathroom. Upstairs is a mezzanine floor with a bedroom and ensuite. The ground floor has a garage, laundry, utilities and guest bedroom plus another living space. This one has more of a man-cave vibe – it's also where the dogs sleep.

The walls are made from reclaimed brick – both from the walls that were demolished to create the courtyard and others purchased for the job. Two tables, one inside and one on the outdoor deck, are made from reclaimed timber that was salvaged from the previous house on this site. Each mismatched plank tells its own story through its colouring and patina.

Elkan sees using reclaimed materials not only as an ethical position but also a practical one. 'I think that it's really important to use reclaimed materials where possible because of the sheer volume of material that is consumed in building. The more that we don't have to extract afresh for each project, the lower the impact that building has on the planet.'

The painted white bricks on the exteriors and timber-lined interiors create an interesting material and aesthetic shift when entering the house. This approach was inspired by Elkan's trips to Japan, where he noted the contrast between outdoor materials and indoor materials on the streets of Tokyo. 'Anywhere you walk around in Tokyo there's these buildings straight to the street, but then these really rich interiors,' he says. 'You walk off the street into this inner world of difference.'

Much of the furniture including built-in seating, is timber, and the timber on the kitchen island is paired with black stone. The ceilings are lined with timber battens and black fabric that provide acoustic and thermal insulation, a solution that Elkan developed with a prior client that is both practical and aesthetically pleasing. The stair is a mix of timber and a cement fibre that brings a soft grey to the palette.

Above: Previously a smash repair shop, the house now has a third storey tucked under the roof.
Right: The exterior's black-and-white scheme contrasts with the timber-lined interiors.

There are many restrictions on what can be done in a heritage area like this, so a lot of time and care was spent making sure that the design complied with all the regulations. The brick walls had to finish at a certain height, so they didn't rise above other buildings in the neighbourhood. The exterior walls were fixed, although the entry now has extra personality due to the addition of a weathered steel panel to the facade above the front door. The roof is corrugated sheet metal to match the rest of the neighbourhood.

With an exterior in hard brick and an interior lined with timber, this house celebrates the honest expression of materials, reflecting Elkan's approach to architecture, which is about trying to improve the way things are done, including material selection. Using timber brings a sense of Japanese design to the property, with a dash of Tom Kundig – a hero to the architect and the client – whose timber-inspired designs were also inspirational here. 'I remember showing [the client] this Tom Kundig book one time and then every time we'd have a discussion we'd say, "That's what Tom Kundig would do",' says Elkan.

Finally, the selection of reclaimed timbers is an important part of what makes this project so sustainable, while retaining its quality and longevity. 'In some instances, reclaimed materials are actually much better than new materials,' says Elkan 'Hardwood is a great example of this. Older hardwood is usually much more stable than freshly cut timber due to its much lower moisture content.' The use of reclaimed bricks in the construction of the third floor and scrap timber to create furniture also exemplifies an approach to design that makes the most of existing materials, juxtaposed with the new.

Timber is the dominant material in the interiors, paired with black,
white and grey.

Top left: View to the courtyard garden.
Bottom left: The upstairs ensuite fits into a small space.

Top right: Timber battens in the bathroom.
Bottom right: Layers of timber in the kitchen.

The main living space has built-in timber furniture running
along one wall.

In the living room, window frames are all made from reclaimed timber.

Top left: View inwards from the deck.
Bottom left: Timber creates vertical and horizontal lines.

Top right: Watching the street from the deck.
Bottom right: The stair in timber and cement fibre.

The many windows and doors to the outdoor spaces are all made
with reclaimed timber.

The creation of outdoor spaces opens the house out to city views.

RECLAIMED: TIMBER DOOR AND WINDOW FRAMES

Although not all the timbers in the house are reused, the doors and windows are 100 per cent reclaimed, sourced from Rob Chapman of Architectural Hardwood Joinery. Chapman has a contract with local demolition people to take all their blackbutt, tallowwood and spotted gum and makes high-quality reclaimed door and window frames from this 100 per cent recycled timber. The timber is cut down to 55 mm – 10 to 15 mm more than other door and window manufacturers – and all the holes in the wood are filled by hand with black epoxy and sanded back. 'He's what I call a true recycler,' say Elkan. 'The windows are made using whichever timbers come. They make a point of leaving holes in the timber rather than sawing or sanding it down to get it perfectly clean, which wastes half of what should be used.'

The doors and windows in Smash Repair House have routed handles, which means that additional hardware is not necessary, keeping the design clean. Details that were required, such as drainage holes and locking strips, are beautifully finished in brass and aluminium respectively. In a house like this, that has a lot of doors and windows, the quality of the timber makes a big difference, and the choice of recycled timber takes the pressure off new timber supply chains. 'Chain of custody, embodied energy, and distance from source are all considerations,' says Elkan. 'On most of these metrics, reclaimed materials are the easiest to justify.'

ARCHITECT	Matt Elkan Architect
PROJECT TEAM	Daina Cunningham, Matt Elkan, Sam Horspool
BUILDER	ARC Projects
ENGINEER	SDA Structures
HERITAGE ARCHITECT	Ruth Daniell
LANDSCAPE DESIGN	Katherine Webster
PHOTOGRAPHY	Clinton Weaver

Above: The view from the deck with black and timber kitchen.

Hachi Lily House

LOCATION	Hue, Vietnam
ARCHITECT	SILAA Architects
REUSED MATERIAL	Timber

SILAA Architects opted for the more affordable option of reclaimed wood over new wood for Hachi Lily House in the village of Thuy Bieu near the centre of the city of Hue, Vietnam. The house was designed for a family of five who decided to move back to their home town from the big city and wanted a tranquil house surrounded by gardens. Hue has become a popular stopping-off point for tourists. It is halfway between Hanoi in the north and Saigon in the south, and is known for a variety of pomelo fruit that is smaller and sweeter than other varieties and grows here in abundance. Thuy Bieu is often called the pomelo village. And so the idea for a small family house nestled in a garden full of pomelo flowers was born. In future, the owners plan to build more on the large 1300 m² site and invite tourists to stay.

    Hachi Lily House is a simple structure with a large living space, kitchen and dining room opening out onto the garden and a waterlily pond at the front of the house. The roof extends past the interiors to shade the front of the house and a verandah where the family can sit together and look out over the pond. Inside, the materials are simple, with wooden walls, ceiling and furniture and a concrete slab floor. Walls clad in grey stone separate this main space from the back part of the house, with bedrooms and bathrooms, and this grey stone is also used on external garden walls to offer privacy for the bedrooms and bathrooms, which open out to the outdoors.

    The choice of timber was made because it is easy to buy, affordable, strong and easy to build with in a short time using local builders. It also makes sense for a house that is connected to nature and will be used to accommodate tourists in the future. In the kitchen, the timber in the bench and table ties the space into one low long line, and there is a picture window above the kitchen. 'The kitchen is a very simple table,' says architect Nguyen Huu Son Duong. 'It's one line with the fridge and the wooden desk, and then we have a window so that you can see through to the garden when you cook.'

    Terracotta tiles have been used on the large sloping roof for functional, aesthetic and financial reasons. 'The gable roof is very normal and simple but I think very effective because we have big rain and harsh sunlight in the summer, so the roof protects the underneath spaces better,' says Nguyen. A mezzanine has been created under the top pitch of the roof with access up a wooden ladder from the main living space. Here there is a storage area as well as a small library with a long narrow skylight. 'On the mezzanine, you can read a book and look out the small window – you can even touch the branch of the pomelo tree through the window,' says Nguyen.

    The main material in this house is timber but there is also concrete for the floor and natural grey stone for some internal and external walls, including those that enclose small courtyards at the back. Brick was used too, plus terracotta tiles for the roof.

Above: The main bedroom in reclaimed timber opens out to a garden screened by a grey stone wall.
Right: The house was built in a garden of pomelo trees with a lily pond at the front.

Hachi Lily House is a celebration of the local. It is a pared-back structure created with local reclaimed materials that honours the pomelo tree, the symbol of this village. And although it has been created with a view to being a homestay for tourists, for now it functions perfectly as a serene and connected home for a family of five.

Left: The bathroom shower opens directly onto a private outdoor space.
Above: The terracotta-tiled roof provides shade for the front porch.

Hachi Lily House

The ground floor is dominated by a large living, dining and kitchen space in reclaimed timber.

Top left: A ladder leads to the top floor.
Bottom left: More timber in the main bedroom.

Top right: The main bedroom has its own private deck.
Bottom right: The bathroom is clad in grey stone.

The kitchen is timber upon timber, while concrete is cool underfoot.

Timber is used for the structure and finish, with the ceilings following
the line of the roof.

RECLAIMED: TIMBER

Reclaimed lumber was used for most of the wood, including the main frame, internal lining, doors and window frames, and internal beams and walls. Internal joinery in the kitchen and much of the furniture is also timber. Nguyen bought the wood at a local shop that collects reclaimed timber from demolished buildings. 'Reclaimed lumber is very popular in the city,' he says. 'We did not use any new wood because it is very expensive and the quality – it's not strong enough.' Reclaimed timber is plentiful, easy to buy and works well for a property that appeals to tourists. The tie-in with nature and the garden with its pomelo trees also makes it the perfect material for this house.

ARCHITECT	SILAA Architects
PROJECT TEAM	Nguyen Huu Son Duong, Nguyen Minh Nhat, Le Nguyen Viet Quan, Nguyen Van Det
PHOTOGRAPHY	Hoang Le

Above: Timber that has aged is stronger and, in Vietnam, it is also cheaper.

Top left: Glazed corner in the bedroom.
Bottom left: View from under the roofline.

Top right: Bed head with integrated shelf.
Bottom right: Grey stone is also used inside.

Ruang Tekuni

LOCATION	Bali, Indonesia
ARCHITECT	DDAP Architect
REUSED MATERIAL	Timber

Above: Reclaimed timber is used extensively in this apartment building.
Right: A historic Chinese house was taken apart, shipped to Bali and reassembled on top of the building.

Built on an empty site in the middle of Kuta in Bali, Ruang Tekuni is a new apartment building built with a variety of different timbers sourced from demolished buildings in Indonesia and neighbouring countries. Designed by Ubud-based architecture practice DDAP, the block is owned by a couple whose business is in reclaimed wood. The owners live in a small home on the top floor of the block. The studio apartments on the levels below are aimed at the expat community, including start-up entrepreneurs and digital nomads. This apartment complex provides an alternative to resort-style accommodation for tourists and local housing.

The architects began with an empty site and started by mapping the surrounding buildings and planning for density, air circulation and sunlight. 'We always start with the context, then from that we factor in the environment,' says I Ketut Dirgantara. Bali is hot and humid all year round, so air circulation was needed to make the building habitable. 'How will the wind enter this building?' Dirgantara asked. 'The design came from maximising wind flow.'

The resulting design brings light and air into the centre of the building by distributing the apartments around a central courtyard and atrium. Wooden walkways on the ground floor and the balconies of the levels above give residents and guests access to breezes, as well as views of a lush tropical garden of plants and a fishpond with gently trickling water.

The 10 apartments are distributed around the courtyard garden on the ground and first levels. A mezzanine level was also created in some of the ground-floor apartments to create more living spaces. At the front of the building, the ground floor is reserved for parking. On the floor above is a swimming pool with a paved seating area.

Although reclaimed timber from old buildings has been used in the interiors, PVC has been used for the pool to keep it as lightweight as possible, combining old and new materials in the build. Elsewhere, the architects used a concrete B-panel insulated with polystyrene that has good acoustic performance. Vertical terracotta tiles with varying degrees of permeability filter light and keep the building cool, and the terracotta tiles on the roof of the new building echo the traditional roof shape of Balinese rice-barns.

On the very top of the whole building is the owners' home. This is not a new build – it is an old Chinese building that was dismantled in China, put into a container and rebuilt on site in Bali. 'This was a request from the client, who said from the beginning, "I have an old Chinese house and the size is this and we need to put it in the design, anywhere you like." I decided to just put it on top of the building,' explains Dirgantara.

The structure of this home, including the roof and walls, are from the old building, but the kitchen and bathroom were constructed new. An elevator was also installed to help the owners access the top floor as they grow older. The house also has space for the owners' private library and workspace. Perched on the top of the new building, it has its own roof garden, which acts as a terrace, leading through to balconies that overlook the courtyard atrium.

Ruang Tekuni is an apartment complex full of paradoxes. This brand-new building celebrates both old and new materials. It has a historic Chinese house that's also a penthouse apartment. And it is a profoundly urban building that is also connected to nature through the tropical jungle garden. For Dirgantara, this garden was the key to designing a happy building: 'Five per cent of your body is how the wind blows, how the water flows and how the light feels,' he says. 'You can feel it like a sense.'

Deck and swimming pool adjacent to the main part of the building.

The swimming pool is on the roof of the parking garage.

Ruang Tekuni

Top left: Detail of a weathered wall.
Bottom left: Peaceful central courtyard.

Top right: Each apartment is unique.
Bottom right: Detail of reclaimed timber and terracotta tiles.

Timber

Top left: Vertical tiles offer ventilation.
Bottom left: Central fish pond and garden.

Top right: Owners' apartment on the top floor.
Bottom right: Reclaimed timber in the stairs.

The historic Chinese house is full of aged timber and furniture pieces.

The roof and walls of the old house were dismantled in China
and reconstructed in Kuta.

Old screens and furniture create layers of reclaimed timber
in the old house.

Retro wooden furnishings in the old house bathroom.

RECLAIMED: TIMBER

Each apartment is fitted out with wooden floors and stairs built from the owner's stash of reclaimed wood. 'They have a huge workshop full of their reclaimed wood,' says Dirgantara. 'The brief was to use as much as possible the wood from their workshop.' While the design of the building was meticulously thought out prior to construction, the finishes were more haphazardly assigned as trucks of lumber arrived.

'I was thinking on the spot. I just used my feeling of sizing, colours, to decide where to put it,' explains Dirgantara. As a result, each apartment was uniquely finished. Some teak was from a badminton court in Jakarta, some from an old building in Java, some came from train tracks, others from buildings as far away as China. Where possible, each type and colour of wood was kept within a single apartment so that the final finish wasn't too irregular. Offcuts were used for things like the finish of stair treads.

ARCHITECT	DDAP Architect
PROJECT TEAM	Dirgantara I Ketut, Yuni Utami Ni Kadek, Iwan, Gunawan, Artha
ENGINEER AND CONSTRUCTION	Unang
LANDSCAPE	Rai Sudjana
PHOTOGRAPHY	DDAP Architect & Sonny Sandjaya

Above: The view from above in one of the new apartments shows the extent of reclaimed timber used.
Right: The stairs in the central courtyard are shaded by perforated terracotta tiles.

MD Apartment

LOCATION	Ahmedabad, India
ARCHITECT	Studio Saransh
REUSED MATERIAL	Timber

When Malay Doshi of Studio Saransh took on the task of designing his own apartment in Ahmedabad, he departed from the new finishes usually used in new residential projects in India, instead opting for reclaimed and handcrafted materials. 'The way people go about it in India is very chic and very finished houses. I didn't want that. I wanted something raw and unfinished on purpose.' The first step was to demolish the existing apartment, including internal partitions, flooring and finishes, and start from scratch. During this time, he lived in the apartment. 'I had a couple of months just to be in the space and think about what I wanted it to become.'

Raw concrete, hand-finished plaster, stone and concrete tiles in grey and blue were juxtaposed with dark, aged teak reclaimed from historic buildings to create a unique material palette. Once the material palette was in place, Doshi could set about designing the space itself, which includes a living room, a raised library space, kitchen, bathroom and bedroom, with storage beyond. The apartment is small, but every centimetre has been planned for functionality and every use has been thought out. 'I always envisioned it as a small space – like getting inside a blanket. It's very cosy.'

Doshi spent a lot of time on site during construction, overseeing the details of the build, including saving offcuts of wood that were later used to line the shelving for shoes near the front door. He even saved a series of slim wooden offcuts and formed them into a grid to make the coffee table. Doshi also brought in several artisans – one to pour the polished concrete, one to hand-finish the plaster and one to work with the stone. This allowed him to become involved in all sorts of details that might not have been possible otherwise. One of his favourites is a brass inlay on the bedside table that shows where a phone can be placed for wireless charging. 'A lot of small things get missed when you design on a computer,' he explains.

This project proves that you don't need to use new materials to create a contemporary design. In fact, sometimes the most contemporary designs are a fusion of old and new. With MD Apartment, Doshi has created a physical connection to our material history through reclaimed materials, while also connecting us to old trades, such as the art of making plaster by hand. These ways of working created a home that is more meaningful than one made with all new materials. And working closely with the builders on site has also resulted in an attention to detail that sets this project apart, creating a cosy home that's also a model of good design.

Above: The shelves for shoes near the front door have been lined in reclaimed timber.
Right: Aged teak timber from demolished buildings forms a central part of the material palette.

Top left: Steps to the raised library area.
Bottom left: Timber scraps were used to make the coffee table.

Top right: Timber offcuts laid into the concrete floor.
Bottom right: Every detail was thought through.

Grey lime plaster was used on the walls to keep the apartment cool.

The kitchen is simple in grey stone and aged teak.

A small library has been created with reclaimed timber shelves
and glass doors.

Top left: Detail of timber and plaster.
Bottom left: Two arches and an arched mirror.

Top right and right: Patterned cement tiles in the bedroom.
Bottom right: Bathroom in black stone and lime plaster.

MD Apartment

View of the main living and dining space from the raised library.

RECLAIMED: TIMBER

Reclaimed timber is an important part of the material palette of MD Apartment, with the dark, aged teak giving it a distinctive look. Doshi found a shop in an industrial part of Ahmedabad that was filled with reclaimed building materials. He bought aged teak that came from housing that dated back to the Mughal Empire, which ended in the mid-1800s. Some of the wood had been carved, glued or had long nails extracted, but it was still stronger than new wood – it had a distinctive look derived from its age. 'Because of the ageing, it gets denser and darker over time,' Doshi explains. 'Some of the pieces of wood had big knots or open gashes – I just used that anyway.'

The use of reclaimed timber in India is slowly becoming more common, a practice led by architects and designers. About 70 per cent of the wood used in MD Apartment is reclaimed and Doshi made sure that it was used in the most efficient way possible, with offcuts kept and reused.

ARCHITECT	Studio Saransh
PROJECT TEAM	Malay Doshi, Arihant Bajaj, Tejashree Karande
PHOTOGRAPHY	Ishita Sitwala, The Fishy Project

Above: Like many woods, teak gets darker and harder as it ages.

Huellas

LOCATION	Madrid, Spain
ARCHITECT	cumulolimbo studio
REUSED MATERIAL	Timber doors, kitchen cabinets and appliances, furniture, metal radiator pylon

Above: The kitchen was moved closer to the entry.
Right: The corridor wall was demolished, but a metal radiator pylon in the wall was retained.

In this tiny apartment in the centre of Madrid, experimental architecture studio cumulolimbo opted not to replace the existing kitchen, but to move it as part of their radical approach to spatial planning and materials use. The owners, a retired couple, had put the kitchen in just 10 years earlier and were happy with it, but the layout of the rest of the apartment, with its underused corridor, large bathroom and tiny bedrooms, was not working for them. The architects also retained a metal radiator pylon that could have been demolished and reused other elements, such as two timber doors and an existing console/shelving furniture unit.

This project is small but radical – characteristic of the work of cumulolimbo, a practice of four women architects that began as a collective when Madrid was ravaged by the economic crisis. The name comes from the idea of a cloud of people – cumulo – working in what architect Natalia Ventura calls 'a middle situation' – limbo. While experimental projects and research were a way to get the studio off the ground, they are now part of the practice's DNA – as is tackling smaller projects such as Huellas apartment. 'What we do is architecture work, not just redecoration,' says Ventura. 'There's architectural processes even if it's a tiny space.'

Built in the 1930s, Huellas is like many apartments of that time. It has large, heated entrances for receiving guests, small bedrooms and inexplicably large bathrooms. The first step was to totally reconfigure the rooms. The wall between the corridor and the living space was removed, creating a large open space for living, dining and kitchen that opens out from the front door. Round windows were cut between this living space and the adjacent rooms and fitted with grid-patterned frosted glass to bring in light but retain privacy.

The kitchen, including cabinets and appliances, was moved 8 metres forward to make way for a small bathroom behind it. New MDF cupboard doors and a splashback in a dark pink triangular tile give the kitchen personality. Ventura refers to the tiles as a 'protagonist material'. The pink colour scheme was extended to the bathroom, where pink tiles were again used, and to the storage in the living space, where MDF cupboard doors were installed to match the kitchen. The pink paint in a simple, handpainted diagonal shape on the MDF was an inexpensive but impactful move. 'We invited a friend of ours who's an artist to paint this salmon colour by hand to create an atmosphere,' says Ventura.

In the main living space, the existing doors were kept, even though they are slightly dated, as they were very good quality wood. For Ventura, these elements are about retaining what is simple. 'The builders said, "Get rid of these doors, they're horrible", but there's a conversation here between the new and the old.' Also reclaimed was an existing piece of sapele timber furniture that was broken up into parts and reassembled in the bedroom as part of the commitment to reuse.

Where the wall was removed, a metal radiator pylon previously located within the wall was retained. This functional item acts as a radiator for heating in the winter and is cool to the touch in summer. It is connected to a suspended steel structure near the ceiling, from which the lights have been hung. This continuation of the metal rod cuts through the space on a diagonal. The ceiling above was left unfinished, and the traces of the prior wall remain, hence the name of the apartment – *huellas* – which means 'traces'.

In the mission to save construction materials going to landfill, even the smallest project has a role to play. With Huellas, Ventura stepped in to rethink the layout of this apartment, on a limited budget, using a creative approach to spatial planning and materials reuse. 'We have this culture where if you buy it new, it's cheaper. If you throw it away, it's cheaper. We have to change this mindset,' says Ventura. 'The planet needs a conscious and respectful way of producing and architecture is a lot about producing. If we can make it possible to renovate a kitchen by moving it, then we are contributing something.'

Above: This existing piece of sapele timber furniture was taken apart and reassembled in the bedroom.

Right: An artist friend painted pink graphics on MDF cupboard doors.

The dark pink tile in the bathroom and kitchen is a 'protagonist material'.

Pink metal mesh elements create storage and tie in with
the pink theme.

Round windows with grid-patterned frosted glass allow light
in but retain privacy.

RECLAIMED: KITCHEN

Rather than pulling out the existing kitchen and sending it to landfill, Ventura asked the builders to move it. This conversation was the most challenging part of the process, says Ventura. 'You have to ask the person who wants to sell you a new kitchen, "Help me to just move all the cupboards and the doors and the stove." You need to have that deeper conversation and reassure them that they are [still] going to earn money.' The old cabinets above head height had new doors added, and the appliances were also moved rather than replaced. 'Reusing and resetting and repair is important for human beings,' says Ventura. 'It's more emotional and it's also about respect for the planet.'

ARCHITECT	cumulolimbo studio
PROJECT TEAM	Natalia Matesanz Ventura
CONSTRUCTION	T&V Soluciones
LOCKSMITH	Luis Hernández
CARPENTRY	Ruaza
PHOTOGRAPHY	Javier de Paz García

Above: Kitchen cupboards and appliances were moved rather than being discarded.

Chelsea Loft

LOCATION	New York, New York, USA
ARCHITECT	Andrew Franz Architect
REUSED MATERIAL	Timber for floors, cabinetry, storage wall and door jambs

Architect Andrew Franz used reclaimed timber extensively in this renovation of a loft apartment in New York's Chelsea, transforming a small space into a bright and comfortable home for four. The building dates from around 1908 and was probably originally a textiles factory. Before the redesign, the apartment was visually and physically closed off. It had a narrow entry bounded by bathroom walls and kitchen counters that restricted circulation and views through to the living space and outside. The owners had lived in the apartment for a number of years, which gave them an understanding of what was needed to make the apartment work for them.

Franz and his team took the design back to basics. They removed all the internal walls and reconfigured the layout to create a big, open space that makes the most of light and views and still honours the geometry of an industrial loft. The entry at the rear of the loft was elevated on a platform, creating a mudroom and a casual lounge and play space that peers out over the main living space. 'The entry dog-leg maximises the flexibility of the home by carving different nooks for different activities and users,' says Franz.

Rather than replacing the demolished walls, room dividers were created using timber cabinets made from reclaimed ash, producing ample space for storage. These were painted in different colours, giving the apartment a sense of vibrancy and energy. The wall of cabinetry dividing the living space from the bedrooms is cobalt blue, and a similar wall of storage in the entry is canary yellow. The client selected the blue, and the architects pushed for the yellow to brighten up the darker part of the apartment near the entry. 'We juxtaposed three different colours of lacquer to define the spaces and introduced colour into what is otherwise a large white industrial box,' says Franz.

These colourful timber storage elements do not reach the ceiling. Instead, they match the height of the kitchen cabinets, creating a consistent line throughout the rooms. Above the blue storage cabinets, steel-framed glass windows allow light from the living room to spill into the bedrooms, maximising daylight and creating a connection between the rooms. Doors of acid-etched glass offer acoustic separation while maintaining a sense of openness and continuity. 'The height of the cabinetry in blue and yellow allowed for visual continuity of the space, as the ceiling and lighting can be seen above, suggesting a larger floor plan,' says Franz. 'It is about bringing daylight into the bedrooms, while making the living room feel like there's more space beyond.'

The plan of this apartment is rational and uses every square inch. The living space contains the kitchen, dining and living room, all flooded with natural light. 'The design takes advantage of the abundant light a corner unit offers and brings it deep into the space,' says Franz.

Above: Blue tiles in the bathroom match the cobalt blue cabinetry made from reclaimed ash.
Right: The new configuration allows views through the apartment to the windows.

There are two small bathrooms, one accessed from the living space and one from the master bedroom. There are no central hallways wasting space and the children's room can be divided into two in the future. There is even a small study nook around the corner from the main living space.

What makes this apartment design so successful are the storage elements that also act as wall dividers. They are functional, separating rooms without closing off the spaces to natural light, and create an impressive amount of storage for an apartment of this size. Importantly, they are also made from reclaimed timber, meaning less use of precious primary materials. And they are colourful, combining the natural beauty of wood with bright blues and yellows. They represent the best of design – a simple but high-impact insertion that works on many levels.

Kitchen cabinets made from reclaimed ash.

Blue and yellow cabinets act as dividing walls.

Glazing above the cabinets allows light to spill over the top.

A raised seating and play area is bounded by a yellow cabinet.

RECLAIMED: TIMBER

Reclaimed timber was used throughout the loft on floors, kitchen cabinets and storage elements, the bathroom ceiling and a built-in sofa. The architect chose reclaimed ash from local supplier The Hudson Company, which sources this hard and structural timber from old New England and Canadian barns. 'It's a beautiful old-growth wood,' says Franz. 'The client had a desire to use wood, and to use as few species as possible. Plus, her husband is Canadian, so this struck a comfortable chord.' Lacquer was used on flat planes of MDF, combining with the natural golden colour of the reclaimed wood to create an appealing finish that also is environmentally friendly.

A sustainable approach to design is also demonstrated through the absence of materials. The industrial character of the apartment was retained, including a bare brick wall behind the kitchen cabinets, and the ceilings were painted white but left exposed, with visible electricals and conduits. This apartment proves that every project, no matter how small, can make a difference by using environmentally friendly materials.

ARCHITECT	Andrew Franz Architect
PROJECT TEAM	Andrew Franz, Greg Clarke
CONSTRUCTION	2K Construction
PHOTOGRAPHY	Albert Vecerka/Esto

Above: The bedrooms are behind the blue cabinet, and can be divided as the children get older.

Rylett House

LOCATION	London, UK
ARCHITECT	Studio 30 Architects
REUSED MATERIAL	Timber floorboards and doors, bricks, recycled terrazzo flooring

This project embodies the spirit of reuse. Split into two maisonettes in the 1970s, Rylett House in Shepherd's Bush, London, has been transformed once again into a single dwelling by Studio 30 Architects. The architects worked collaboratively with the couple who own it – interior designer Helen Arvanitakis and structural engineer Tom Steel. Many of the decisions were made on site, meaning that materials could be taken up, assessed and reused where possible. This includes the bricks from demolished walls, timber floorboards that were taken up, oiled and relaid, and all the existing internal timber doors, which were moved to accommodate a new floor plan.

This is the second Shepherd's Bush house that Studio 30 has worked on with the owners, so friendship and trust already existed between architect, interior designer and engineer. The floor plan had to be substantially altered to convert two separate flats into one resolved house, with living rooms converted to bedrooms, and vice versa, on both floors.

The most significant change was on the ground floor, where the existing kitchen and dining with glass conservatory attached has been totally replaced with one large room that features an open kitchen and dining space. A huge skylight above the kitchen brings in light, and the new exterior walls are made of reclaimed bricks taken from elsewhere in the property. The floor above has been extended on the southern half of this new room below to form a new bedroom and ensuite. On both floors, the bay windows at the front of the house that are common in Victorian-era buildings like this, are now used in the main living room downstairs and main bedroom upstairs.

Reclaimed timber was used throughout the house in the flooring, but without completely resanding them and losing the patina of the wood. The team also worked very hard to reclaim the old staircase. The staircase was moved and extended to the loft and around the basement. Where there were not enough spindles, new ones were created that matched the old, and the handrail is a collection of old and new pieces. 'It's not necessarily the most economical way of doing things but for the client it was very important to keep the history of the house,' says Henri Bredenkamp from Studio 30 Architects. Internal timber doors were also reused, even though their style was very different to that of the new house, and a lot of work was done to make sure they fitted physically into the layout.

The rear doors were made of larch and were made unusually large. 'Doors of that size could bow and warp, but it was good to work with Tom who was happy to risk it, to a certain extent,' says Bredenkamp. 'He was able to trust his own skills as a structural engineer.' Other recycled materials include the terrazzo flooring in the main kitchen and dining room.

The combination of contemporary design with a heritage building works beautifully in this house. This has been achieved through Bredenkamp's expertise, Arvanitakis's

Above: A conservatory at the back on the ground floor has been replaced with a new extension.
Right: The extension has unusually large rear doors made with larch.

choice of furniture and Steels's confidence to take risks. The main kitchen and dining space is a wonderful example of this – the mismatched modern chairs at the dining table speak of new design, a beautifully worn carpenter's bench has been transformed into a kitchen island, and the huge larch doors take the structure to its engineering limits.

A willingness to make quick decisions about the use of materials during the build gave the architecture, design and engineering team the ability to use far more reclaimed materials than is normally possible. The use of terrazzo in the main kitchen and dining space was a stroke of genius, creating a hard-wearing surface that is also made partially from recycled materials. In Rylett House, reuse has been the rule, rather than being a one-off decision for one material. The result is a contemporary design with the benefit of the patina that comes with reused materials.

Rylett House

The new kitchen dining space has recycled terrazzo flooring
and a selection of designer chairs.

The kitchen island is a repurposed carpenter's bench.

Timber floorboards were lightly sanded and sealed to retain
their patina.

Reclaimed timber floors are paired with a dark wall in the study.

The ensuite has an almost comic-book style with black grout
and fittings and a canary yellow wall.

Bay windows were retained in the bedroom, which was formerly
a living room.

RECLAIMED: TIMBER FLOORS

Throughout Rylett House, the existing timber hardwood has been reused as much as possible. The benefits of using 100-year-old wood are that it doesn't move the way new hardwood does. 'Normally when you do underfloor heating you need engineered floorboards because they're more dimensionally stable,' explains Bredenkamp. 'But if you actually use timber which is hundreds of years old it's done its movement.' The floorboards were not sanded back, as that would have resulted in the loss of grain and patina accumulated over many years. Instead, they had a light sand and a neutral stain. 'A lot of the character of the board is still readable,' says Bredenkamp.

For Studio 30, reclaimed materials are a good way to bridge contemporary and heritage design. When converting historic building styles into a contemporary aesthetic, the patina of worn materials is less jarring than completely new materials. Also, many of their clients are interested in having an eco-friendly house. 'I'm relatively fortunate that my projects are houses for people and most of my clients are actually interested in the planet or [at least] in the longer-term running costs of the building,' says Bredenkamp.

ARCHITECT	Studio 30 Architects
PROJECT TEAM	Henri Bredenkamp
INTERIOR DESIGNER	Helen Arvanitakis
CONTRACTOR	Cornerstone Contractors
STRUCTURAL ENGINEER	Heyne Tillett Steel
FIRE CONSULTANT	Fire Risk Solutions
BUILDING INSPECTOR	London Building Control
PHOTOGRAPHY	Agnese Sanvito

Above: Oversized larch windows in an upper-storey bedroom offer garden views.
Left: The existing timber staircase was retained and extended.

Following pages, Left: Metal film-room doors create a sense of history at Crate Apartment.
Right (inset): Metal bath in the Casey House bathroom.
Right (border): Reclaimed metal door at Crate Apartment.

FILMS
SMOKING &
NAKED LIGHTS
PROHIBITED

NO
ADMITTANCE
PROJECTION
ROOM

METAL

18.6 MJ

The production of 1 kilogram of steel for construction requires 18.6 megajoules of energy.

Vassart, Olivier & Cajot, Louis-Guy, 'Sustainability of buildings made of steel', Meed Conference on Environment, Dubai, January 2009, <researchgate.net/publication/278673238_Sustainability_of_buildings_made_of_steel>.

20.4 Mt

In 2017, the Australian construction and demolition industry generated 20.4 million tonnes of waste, including bricks, concrete, metal, timber, plasterboard, asphalt, rock and soil.

Shooshtarian, Salman, Wong, Peter, Yang, Rebecca & Maqsood, Tayyab, 'We create 20m tons of construction industry waste each year. Here's how to stop it going to landfill', *The Conversation*, 19 July 2019, <theconversation.com/we-create-20m-tons-ofconstruction-industry-waste-each-year-heres-how-to-stop-it-going-to-landfill-114602>.

40%

Construction creates an estimated one-third of the world's overall waste and at least 40 per cent of the world's carbon dioxide emissions.

Miller, Norman, 'The industry creating a third of the world's waste', *Future Planet*, BBC, 16 December 2021, <bbc.com/future/article/20211215-the-buildings-made-from-rubbish>.

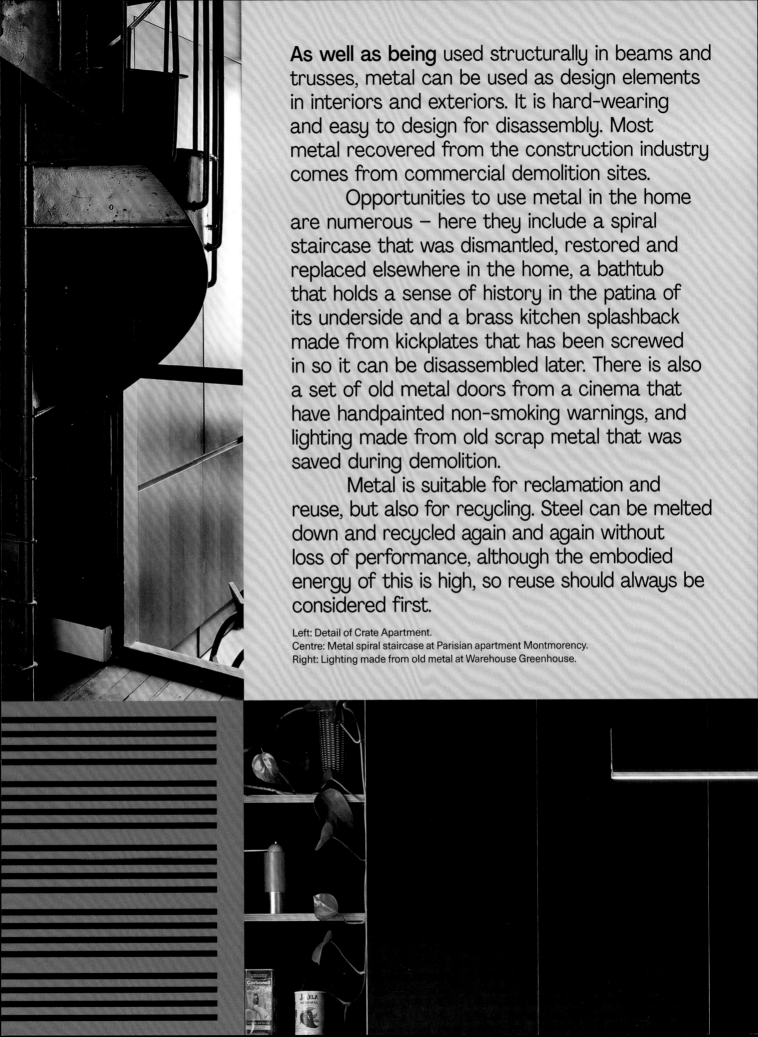

As well as being used structurally in beams and trusses, metal can be used as design elements in interiors and exteriors. It is hard-wearing and easy to design for disassembly. Most metal recovered from the construction industry comes from commercial demolition sites.

Opportunities to use metal in the home are numerous – here they include a spiral staircase that was dismantled, restored and replaced elsewhere in the home, a bathtub that holds a sense of history in the patina of its underside and a brass kitchen splashback made from kickplates that has been screwed in so it can be disassembled later. There is also a set of old metal doors from a cinema that have handpainted non-smoking warnings, and lighting made from old scrap metal that was saved during demolition.

Metal is suitable for reclamation and reuse, but also for recycling. Steel can be melted down and recycled again and again without loss of performance, although the embodied energy of this is high, so reuse should always be considered first.

Left: Detail of Crate Apartment.
Centre: Metal spiral staircase at Parisian apartment Montmorency.
Right: Lighting made from old metal at Warehouse Greenhouse.

Montmorency

LOCATION	Paris, France
ARCHITECT	Camille Hermand Architectures
REUSED MATERIAL	Metal spiral staircase, timber beams for ceilings and walls, tiles, parquet floors, kitchen

This heritage 19th-century apartment in Paris has been transformed by Camille Hermand Architectures by making use of existing materials, including a beautiful spiral staircase that was taken apart, stripped down to its steel structure and reconstructed as a feature that speaks to the history of the home. Montmorency is in one of the oldest streets of the historic Marais district, adjacent to the Duke of Montmorency's mansion, from which it takes its name. It is the home of architect Camille Hermand and her three children.

Hermand first purchased the ground floor of this property, which was previously a jewellery boutique, to use as an office. When the opportunity to buy the apartment above arose, she converted it into her own home. Now, with her family growing and her business requiring a new space, Hermand has found new offices elsewhere and converted both floors into a two-level family home. This makes this the third project in the same space – her office, an office with a home above, and a single residence. 'There were three different times and three different ways of using this place,' she explains. 'Each one has been rich in good moments and good ideas.'

'The kitchen was first installed upstairs and then moved downstairs,' says Hermand. 'My marble worker hated me.' One of the kitchen walls was stripped back to its ancient timber vertical beam structure to bring in light and air circulation. An old storage closet is now the pantry. The living room is also downstairs, connected to the kitchen.

Next to this, what was the office meeting space is now a mini-library with table and chairs for homework and art projects. One wall has a floor-to-ceiling bookcase with teal-green storage cupboards underneath, and the adjacent wall features patterned wallpaper that looks like it has been block-printed in blues and greens. On the wall beside this, original cream wall tiles have been kept intact, complete with imperfections, and there is a row of chocolate-brown feature tiles near the top where a hat rack has been installed.

Upstairs, a vestibule has been built around the top of the spiral staircase with windows through to one of the bedrooms. Four bedrooms and two bathrooms are cleverly arranged around a central circulation space, with interior windows creating a sense of transparency and bringing light into the centre of the space. What used to be the living room is now the master bedroom, and the tiny former kitchen space is now a second bathroom. The first bathroom has not been touched.

As a result of this apartment's unique evolution, the designers have used three reuse strategies. First, reusing furniture and lighting from the previous project, much of which was vintage to begin with and bought from local flea markets. Second, making the most of the historic building's existing materials, such as timber beams to ceiling and walls, old tiles

Above: An upstairs bedroom has windows that look onto the spiral staircase.
Right: A former meeting room is now a dining room with built-in library wall.

that have been left untouched, parquet floors and a metal spiral staircase that was taken apart and then lovingly restored. And third, the relocation rather than replacement of the existing kitchen. All three strategies make this a total reduce, reuse and recycle project.

Above: A wall opening in the kitchen was created with timber vertical beams left intact.

Right: A former office is now an open living space, dining room and kitchen.

Top left: Old tiles from when this was a dairy market.
Bottom left: Master bedroom with exposed beams.

Top right: Bathroom from the previous renovation
Bottom right: Detail of the bookcase.

Metal

Top left: Curated finds from the flea market.
Bottom left: This bathroom replaces a tiny kitchen.

Top right: Green-and-blue patterned wallpaper.
Bottom right: Olive green entry walls.

Above: The main bedroom is one of four on the upper floor and was previously the living room.

Right: The living room features warm colours and an eclectic range of furniture.

RECLAIMED: METAL SPIRAL STAIRCASE

The metal spiral staircase was installed not long after the apartment was built. It dates to the beginning of the 20th century. Typical of old Parisian apartments, it was used by the ground-level shop to access the storeroom on the floor above. When Hermand first bought Montmorency, the staircase was covered in carpet. In the first redesign, she painted it, but decided for this latest renovation that it would be more interesting to show the original patina. The placement was also wrong. To make the best use of the new layout of this two-floor apartment, Hermand dismantled and removed the staircase, then replaced it in a different orientation. 'The staircase changed position twice: as it is a spiral, it was easy to make it rotate to give it the best possible position according to the configurations,' says Hermand. The historic layers of paint were removed to show the patina of the original metal, an aesthetic that ties in perfectly with the aged timber of the beams in the wall beside it.

ARCHITECT	Camille Hermand Architectures
PROJECT TEAM	Camille Hermand
STYLIST	Véronique Villaret
PHOTOGRAPHY	Hervé Goluza

Above: The kitchen was moved downstairs instead of being completely replaced.

Metal

The staircase was taken apart, stripped back and reassembled.

Casey House

LOCATION	Austin, Texas, USA
ARCHITECT	Side Angle Side
REUSED MATERIAL	Metal bath; timber (various) for beams, floors, barn door, shelves and bench; lighting in the living room and bathroom

Reclaimed materials were always going to be an important part of Casey House, thanks to owner and architectural photographer Casey Dunn's penchant for collecting found materials and objects. One house in the nearby district of Red River was said to be a hangout of Bob Dylan's guitarist, Charlie Sexton. It was so full of history and charm that Dunn looked into having it moved wholesale to a new location. When this wasn't possible, he asked Arthur Furman and Annie-Laurie Grabiel to design a new house full of old materials, including some retrieved from the Red River house.

The site is an interesting one. Prior to Casey House being built on the land, there was only one small building on it. It was off to the side and functioned as a small art gallery with a residence above. Most of the block remained a large, empty lawn, which was often used for art parties. The architects realised that the land was large enough to build a new house on, while also retaining the existing building. That structure is now used as the Dunn photography studio and as rented studio space for another artist.

As well as his love for reclaimed materials, Dunn also brought to the project a passion for Marfa Modernism – a style of architecture that originated in the Texan town of Marfa and is known for its minimalism and honest materials, often set on the backdrop of the stark desert. When Casey House was being designed, Dunn was photographing a book called *Marfa Modern* and this style became an important reference point. 'We also share an interest and affinity for west Texas and Marfa,' says Furman. 'That part of the state is just so epic. It's like another world. There is poetry in the simplicity.'

Part of the Marfa influence came in the look of the exterior. It is not exactly adobe but has a monolithic presence in burnished grey stucco. In profile, the shape of the house is a simple box with a gable roof that is nearly flush with the side walls, giving an impression of a home drawn by a child. 'The project was definitely an exercise in proportion – if it got too wide it looked funny, if it got too tall it looked funny,' says Grabiel. The shape also fit with the Marfa influence. 'The style of architecture is rough, it's rustic. It's a basic form of architecture.'

The house design packs a lot into a small footprint. The side entry opens into a short entry hall that leads to the centre of the house, where a staircase rises. To the right, two bedrooms and a family bathroom are tucked out of sight, and to the left, the house opens to a large kitchen, dining and living space with double-height ceiling and views out to the garden. 'One thing that's common with older houses that are built here is to put all the bedrooms at the back of the house and the living at the front and kitchen at the side, but then there's

Above: From the driveway, the house looks like a child's drawing in grey stucco.
Right: A deck at the side of the house offers an outdoor dining option.

no way of getting from the living spaces to the backyard,' says Furman. 'So we started this project with the opposite in mind.'

The concrete wall that screens the entry hall is also the kitchen splashback, and the staircase is open to the living room, making the most of the double-height ceilings. Upstairs, the plate height has been lowered to keep the profile of the house small. There are gabled ceilings in the master bedroom and a reclaimed barn door leads to the small bathroom. This sliding door was full of nail holes when it was salvaged. It was split lengthways and put together using a butterfly joint, giving it even more character.

Reclaimed materials are throughout the house, including a metal bath, longleaf pine for the floors and timber for beams, barn door, shelves and benches, as well as hanging lights in the living room and light fixtures in the main bathroom.

The house also has good passive design, thanks to its orientation, which minimises western and eastern exposure and allows cross-ventilation. It adheres to Texan energy codes, which are some of the strictest in the United States. It has solar panels with battery backups and charging facilities for an electric car, and the roof of the studio collects rainwater in an above-ground cistern. This efficient design has taken every step to be as sustainable as possible, including the use of reclaimed materials.

Casey House

Side Angle Side designed the house so that the living spaces look
out onto the garden.

The kitchen is open plan, with a grey wall dividing it from the entry.

Above: Timber flooring throughout is reclaimed pine.

Right: The staircase to the upstairs rooms overlooks the living room, with old timber beams overhead.

RECLAIMED: METAL BATH

The metal bath in the master bedroom was retrieved by
Dunn from the Red River house. Rather than building the
bath in, the architects left it freestanding, and placed it
on pine blocks. The blocks – along with much of the pine
in the house – were salvaged from an old warehouse.
'He's such a collector of found things and reclaimed things,'
says Furman. 'He already had a good collection of random
old pieces of wood or planks or things he'd been stashing
and storing.' In the end, it brought a character to Casey
House that could not have been achieved otherwise.
'In early design conversations, we discussed how to make
a brand-new house feel like it's been there already – it has
that character of an older home,' says Grabiel.

ARCHITECT	Side Angle Side
PROJECT TEAM	Arthur Furman, Annie-Laurie Grabiel
INTERIOR DESIGN	Ann Edgerton
BUILDER	Waller Building Company
STRUCTURAL ENGINEER	GreenEarth Engineering
LANDSCAPE DESIGN	Studio Balcones
LIGHTING DESIGN	Paterson Electric
PHOTOGRAPHY	Casey Dunn

Above: The sliding door to the ensuite is made of two pieces
of old timber.

The bath is from a local house famous for being a hangout
of Bob Dylan's guitarist, Charlie Sexton.

Rooftop Home

LOCATION	London, UK
INTERIOR DESIGNER	Retrouvius
REUSED MATERIAL	Brass kickplates; lighting; terrazzo columns; timber (various) for cladding, doors, shelves, cupboard fronts and drawers; limestone; marble

Reclamation is not a new thing for Adam Hills and Maria Speake. They met studying architecture at the Glasgow School of Art in the late 1980s, where they were horrified to see the destruction that is routine in the construction industry. In 1993 they set up Retrouvius, a salvage and interior design business, and now have a warehouse full of incredible salvaged materials, architectural details and objects. Hills runs the salvage side of the business and Speake leads an interior design team whose projects demonstrate how beautiful salvage can be. When they decided to renovate and redesign their own home in London's Marylebone, they used their extensive experience of working with reclaimed materials to get the best results, while also testing out a few new ideas.

Adam's father, architect Nicholas Hills, designed this apartment originally. It was built on the roof of York House, a five-storey block of Edwardian mansion flats. Adam Hills grew up in the apartment, which had an L-shaped open-plan design and a distinctive brown-and-white check pattern on the carpets, curtains and tiling. In the 1990s, Hills and Speake moved in with their young children. But the open plan that had worked so well when the children were small did not offer enough privacy to a family with teenagers. 'Not a single person could slam a door in frustration or close themselves away for privacy,' says Speake. 'The bathroom was behind a curtain. It was marvellously bohemian and great for parties – and great when the kids were little. But for teenage-dom, people need to have their own zones to develop and extend in their own way.'

Speake set about redesigning the apartment. The first step was to divide the large open-plan kitchen and dining room into two rooms, creating a new entry hall where the kitchen once was and separating it from the dining room both physically and visually. Key to this was the insertion of an incredible salvaged piece – a row of fluted terrazzo columns from Lewis's department store in Liverpool that dated back to the 1930s. 'With Nicholas's original design, it looked like a hallway, but it never functioned like that – you ended up walking straight into the kitchen. There was never a sense of "Hi, can I take your coat?",' explains Speake. 'A decompression area. Hallways are quite nice. And the whole space feels bigger when it's been divided.'

The new dining room is dominated by a beautiful 1950s tapestry in gold and red designed by French tapestry artist Jean Lurcat, and there is vintage furniture everywhere. The kitchen has been moved to a small space next to the dining room that was previously part of the open-plan living space. It is dominated by brass and timber. The splashback is made from old brass kickplates and most of the cupboard fronts, including the lower and full-length timber doors, are salvaged iroko, a

tropical hardwood that was used in schools and science labs throughout Britain in the early 20th century. Above these, the cupboards are fronted with frames that once housed the textile archive of London's V&A museum. 'Most kitchens have high-level cupboards that are too deep, so I always loved these, which are the depth of a cereal box,' says Hills. 'We've flipped the backs to show the texture and specific loan details handwritten for each one.'

A variety of different reclaimed timbers are used throughout the project. Reclaimed copper light doors (glazed doors with painted copper in a grid pattern on the glass) have been installed between the entry hall and the study. They were designed by British architect Edwin Lutyens and come from a commercial building in London. The study has leather panels taken from the old British Library, some of the joinery is fronted with timbers from the former UK Patent Office, and the shelving was made from poplar and oak. Reclaimed teak that was originally used as flooring in a London museum was used as exterior cladding and in the bathroom.

'The thing we loved about the teak is we could just re-oil it,' says Hills. 'It has an unbelievable longevity. The previous pine cladding had been up there for 40 years, and this teak is double the thickness and is a tropical hardwood.'

Unusual details of the original architecture have been retained, including a round corner turret that now is the main bedroom ensuite, as well as several small bedrooms with timber loft ceilings that the family calls the 'cabins'. Some of these rooms have been refinished with reclaimed materials, including one that now has reclaimed maple strip flooring from a school assembly hall, and another that has pine floorboards and matching bed frames with drawers that are made from pine that was previously used for storing maturing cheeses.

One of the benefits of owning one of London's best-known salvage businesses is that you find out about amazing materials. The main family bathroom is lined with limestone rich in crinoid (ancient sea fossils) that was originally the concourse flooring of the Terminal 2 building at Heathrow Airport. Pink marble in the main ensuite comes from the foyer of a 1970s bank in central London.

For Speake, being both the designer and the client on Rooftop Home was not easy, but it did give her the opportunity to use knowledge she has gained from other projects about using reclaimed materials, while also creating the chance to experiment. For her, salvage is not about the look, it is a way of thinking, a way of designing. 'We need to value every little piece of what we extract or create,' she says. 'Because morally it feels like the most important and right thing to do.'

In the mission to use more reclaimed materials in construction, Rooftop Home is an exemplar. The project prioritises the value of materials, finding inventive ways to reuse each one and, in doing so, making them fashionable again. For Speake, the worst thing would be to recreate the *look* of salvage without the environmental benefit. The attention to detail in this home is outstanding. Each surface tells stories of architectural history and everyday use.

Previous page: The former studio overlooking the rooftop garden is now the main living room.

Above: The living room features a Feuille de Choux tapestry from the 16th century.

Top left: Worn leather-fronted joinery.
Bottom left: Window seat with rooftop views.

Top right: Green sofa and reclaimed timber.
Bottom right: Storage in the bedroom.

Fluted terrazzo columns create an entry hallway.

The columns were retrieved from a department store in Liverpool
and date back to the 1930s.

View through to the dining room with skylight above.

A stunning Jean Lurçat tapestry dominates the dining room.

The stylish main bedroom with ensuite in the round corner turret.

Top left: Top kitchen cupboards are from the V&A Museum.
Bottom left: Vaulted bedroom ceilings.

Top right: Bedrooms are in the 'cabins'.
Bottom right: Detail of the study.

RECLAIMED: BRASS KICKPLATES

Brass kickplates were screwed into the kitchen wall to form a splashback, creating a practical and functional use for an otherwise waste material that also looks fresh and new. 'What we're trying to do is make the unfashionable and rejected fashionable again,' Speake says. 'Or at least relevant and interesting. Sometimes it's just reusing it, sometimes it's reusing it in a different place.' These kickplates are a durable material that can simply be screwed to the wall and unscrewed later to be reused in another project. They can go back to being kickplates or skirting, clad a door or frame a mirror.

The ultimate in salvage, explains Speake, is also being aware that the material should be deconstructed and salvaged again in the future. It should not be cut into smaller pieces than necessary or installed in a way that makes it necessary to destroy it to remove it. 'When things get smaller it's hard to find its reuse,' says Speake. 'Good quality materials are more likely to be used in future.'

INTERIOR DESIGNER	Retrouvius
PROJECT TEAM	Maria Speake, Adam Hills
PHOTOGRAPHY	Theodore Tennant

Above: The brass panels are simply screwed into the wall.
Left: The kitchen features brass kickplates reinvented as a splashback.

Crate Apartment

LOCATION	Singapore
INTERIOR ARCHITECTURE	UPSTRS_
REUSED MATERIAL	Metal doors

Two reclaimed metal doors from an old cinema add a sense of history to Crate Apartment in Singapore, a project otherwise dominated by concrete and plywood. The design strategy by UPSTRS_ centred around the removal of all non-structural internal walls and the insertion of a timber box or 'crate' in the centre of the space, creating a centre of timber ply surrounded by a perimeter of pale grey concrete.

The owners had worked with the architects on two previous residences. This project was much bigger – they wanted to renovate a 1980s apartment (large for Singaporean public housing) that was previously divided into a rabbit warren of small rooms. 'The living room, dining room and kitchen were compartmentalised into isolated rooms, connected by a narrow linear corridor,' explains architect Dennis Cheok. 'This is a reflection of the typical Asian lifestyle in the 1980s, where the daily running of the household and the kitchen is shielded away from the front-facing spaces for guests.'

The apartment had to be totally changed to accommodate 21st century life. The design team went with an unconventional and dramatic approach. All non-structural walls were removed from the apartment to create an almost completely open-plan space, and new rooms were created thanks to an ingenious insertion into the heart of the space – a huge timber box.

This radical move was in part inspired by the owners, who had seen an image of a red shipping container in the centre of a house and showed it to the design team. 'We looked into that particular project, and quickly realised that the image was a clever illusion,' says Cheok. But the image sparked an idea. 'Our immediate response was, "How about building an actual 'box', right in the centre of your home?".'

The new layout, designed for the family of three plus a live-in domestic helper, includes a master bedroom with walk-in closet and ensuite bathroom, a child's bedroom and guest bedroom, an open kitchen with dining table for 10 people, a separate Asian kitchen, a living room and plenty of storage.

Because of the way the timber crate is positioned in the centre of the space, the materiality of each room depends on where it is on the plan. The kitchen and living room are part of the grey concrete 'edge', and the bedrooms feature timber joinery towards the centre of the apartment, and concrete and glazing on their perimeter. The joinery also acts as storage and room divider, neatly hiding away much of the stuff of living and allowing the rest of the apartment to remain monochromatic and minimalist.

The materials used in this apartment renovation are simple: joinery from raw, unadorned plywood for the central 'box' and exposed cement screed for the architectural shell. Two metal doors, found in a junk shop, celebrate the cinematic history of the local area, and a piece of timber inserted into the stone kitchen benchtop is also reclaimed. This is a board used

Above: Detail of the dressing room off the bedroom.
Right: Old metal doors add character to the concrete and timber apartment.

for making popiah – a type of Singaporean spring roll – and is a nod to the family's popiah parties. The design team also designed and built a child's bed with removeable panels so it can transition from a small cot to a larger bed as he gets older.

The idea of creating a box in a box – a timber box within a concrete apartment – is what makes this apartment distinctive. This is supported by a radical approach to materials that reduces everything to plywood and concrete. Within this framework, the insertion of two metal doors that have a fascinating history, as well as the popiah board, create objects of narrative interest that are built into the fabric of the apartment, creating talking points and a sense of connection to culture.

'Being part of the building industry that contributes so much to the consumption of materials and its wastage, using less to achieve more can be the most succinct form of sustainability,' says Cheok. 'As a design studio, finding new meanings through the usage of reclaimed materials can bring so much meaning and nuance that is hard to replicate with modern materials.'

Crate Apartment

To the left is all concrete and to the right is the timber 'crate'.

The timber box converts the big open space into rooms.

Bedrooms feature a mix of timber and concrete.

The theme continues into the master bedroom.

Crate Apartment

RECLAIMED: METAL DOORS

The two reclaimed metal film-room doors installed on one corner of the timber box in Crate Apartment were found in a junk shop. They were salvaged from Singapore's Capitol Theatre, which was built in 1929, and tell the story of their nearly 100 years of use. One door reads in handpainted words 'Films, smoking and naked lights prohibited' and 'No admittance projection room' in cream paint on black, and the other door is a dirty green colour with red and white letters that read 'No smoking, no admittance'. Both doors are patinated and feature studs, peeling paint and metal clasps. As well as being talking points, the doors create an added sense of connection for the owners, who both work in the broadcast industry and are avid film fans. 'It seemed like a meaningful backstory,' says Cheok. 'Serendipity can play a huge role in shaping the design process sometimes. It was a thrill for [the owners] to own a little part of Singapore's cultural history in their very own home.'

INTERIOR ARCHITECTURE	UPSTRS_
PROJECT TEAM	Dennis Cheok, Chong Xiao Ran
BUILDER	RSID Interiors
STYLIST	Betty Wong
PHOTOGRAPHY	UPSTRS_ and Wong Weiliang

Above: The metal doors are not functional but are full of character.
Right: As well as defining spatial zones, the timber 'box' also creates ample storage.

Warehouse Greenhouse

LOCATION	Melbourne, Australia
INTERIOR ARCHITECTURE	Breathe
REUSED MATERIAL	Steel for lighting, timber kitchen benchtops, terrace decking

This warehouse conversion by Breathe in the inner-Melbourne suburb of Brunswick was designed to improve thermal performance by using passive-house methodologies. It was also about doing more with less, achieved through the adaptive reuse of an existing building, the salvaging of demolition materials from site and the use of reclaimed, sustainable and low-embodied-energy materials.

The owners met the architects through a local community reforestation project. They had been living in the converted 1960s warehouse for a couple of years, but the lack of insulation in the building had resulted in some bitterly cold winters. Passionate about the environment and keen to transform the space into a comfortable family home, they hired an architecture practice well known for its creative approach to sustainable design. 'The clients were really like-minded on this project,' says Madeline Sewall from Breathe Architecture. 'They are interested in passive-house methodology and care deeply about the environment.'

The first step was to demolish the roof and replace it with a roofline that makes space for a new mezzanine floor and opens the terrace to the sky above.

The new design has three levels. On the ground floor, there is an entry area, an artist's studio (the owner makes jewellery), a garage, a toilet and utility spaces. The first floor is the main living space and has a large open room with kitchen and enclosed pantry at the back opening to an above-ground terrace. The terrace was created by demolishing the roof, but the walls of the original building were retained and act as a windbreak. On the mezzanine second floor are three bedrooms and a bathroom, and one of the bedrooms has a loft bed – a mezzanine on the mezzanine.

The intention to salvage and reuse started with the demolition of the roof. Pieces of steel were saved and reused in the strip pendant lighting in the kitchen, bathroom and stairs. Timber roof purlins were also saved, remilled and used as benchtops in the kitchen and bathroom, and as stair treads. The blackened edges of the timber show the history of the building – a fire charred them at some point in the past. The terrace decking is recycled ironbark timber.

Materials were retained from the existing structure, and – where possible – not refinished. The concrete floors come from the original building and have been lightly cleaned up. The original blond brick structure has been retained in its raw and unfinished beauty, and the steel windows in the kitchen and living room have also been kept. The black steel structural trusses, including those that once held the roof, have also been retained.

Instead of changing the existing building, the design strategy was to build a new thermal envelope inside, using insulated walls, double-glazed windows and air-tightness membranes. Walls were thickened to around 400 mm and fitted with a heat recovery and ventilation system or trickle ventilation system that has an in-line fan and ceramic honeycomb. This system maintains good air quality by exhausting CO_2, and has been used in conjunction with excellent air-tightness and insulation to eliminate the need for heating or air-conditioning.

The terrace floor has also been built up to insulate the floor below. This platform has been brought partly into the living space to create a seat-height bench and blur the boundaries between outside and inside. The ground-floor entry has also been insulated, creating not only a thermal efficiency, but also an acoustic relief from the busy street. It is a space to take off your shoes and transition to the inside. This was inspired by the Japanese idea of a *genkan* entry and includes plywood shelving for storing shoes.

The floor of the new mezzanine was created in yellow tongue timber, a health-and-safety requirement, but instead of being refinished, it was sealed in oil. On the walls, instead of using plasterboard, which has a high embodied energy, the interior lining is either a local FSC-certified form ply, whitewashed so you can still see the grain, or a fibre-cement sheet. The bathrooms feature brick tiles that have a lower embodied energy than ceramic tiles.

All the windows are now double-glazed, and thanks to the insulation throughout the house, the entire envelope is airtight, according to passive-house principles. In the main kitchen–dining space, the windows are operable – not for cross-ventilation, which is provided by the trickle ventilation system, but so that the owners can tend to the plants in window boxes outside that give this project its name.

Other new materials used in the project were selected for their eco-friendly characteristics, including 100 per cent recyclable, black, hot-rolled mild steel, used in the kitchen splashback and metal components of kitchen and bathroom joinery, and raw brass tapware instead of chrome-plated. The external cladding is 100 per cent recyclable zincalume. Energy is provided by a solar photovoltaic array and connection to 100 per cent certified green power, and water comes from a rainwater capture and reuse tank.

'Reducing embodied energy in construction is so important, which is why we've used adaptive reuse to improve the built fabric that we already have in our city, instead of breaking things down and sending them to landfill,' says Sewall. As well as showing the value in adapting existing buildings, this project also shows that a big change can be made to a building without the excessive use of materials. Each architectural insertion has been carefully chosen for maximum contribution to the comfort of the home and minimum impact on the environment. Warehouse Greenhouse is a case study in restraint.

Right: A new roof was built to create an extra storey.

The metal structure throughout is a unifying feature.

The walls of the outdoor deck were retained to offer privacy
and a windbreak.

White walls balance the heaviness of the black metal.

Metal

Top left: Carbon neutral bricks in the bathroom.
Bottom left: Windows open out onto a kitchen garden.

Top right: Parts of the existing brick walls remain untouched.
Bottom right: Raw chrome taps last longer than chrome-plated.

Warehouse Greenhouse

RECLAIMED: STEEL FOR LIGHTING

Steel reclaimed from the demolition of the roof was used
to create strip pendant lights. 'This light was made from
a wall tie that came down in demolition,' says Sewall. 'We
were able to use it in the light fixtures in the kitchen and
behind the stair.' Reclaimed materials, either salvaged from
demolition on site or purchased elsewhere, are part of
this 'do more with less' strategy. 'We're in the middle of a
climate and biodiversity crisis,' says Sewall. 'Unfortunately,
the government isn't leading the way on regulations and
demanding better from the built environment, so I think
it's up to architects to champion that and to demonstrate
leadership by prioritising it and educating clients about it
as well. Each client then has their sphere of influence too.'

ARCHITECT	Breathe
PROJECT TEAM	Jeremy McLeod, Madeline Sewall, Daniel McKenna, Renee Jacovides, Sarah Mealy
CONSTRUCTION	Never Stop Group
STRUCTURAL ENGINEER	Keith Long and Associates
ECOLOGICALLY SUSTAINABLE DEVELOPMENT CONSULTANT	Nick Bishop ESD
BUILDING SURVEYOR	Metro Building Surveying
LAND SURVEYOR	Webster Survey Group
PHOTOGRAPHY	Tom Ross

Above: Lights above the kitchen island are made from salvaged
metal from the roof.
Right: The salvaged timber used in the benchtop has charred
edges from a historic fire.

Following pages, Left: Recycled kitchen cabinets and benchtop
at Mountain View.
Right (inset): Recycled plastic in the orange and blue window
seat at Mountain View.
Right (border): The blue room with salvaged plasterwork
at Mountain View.

RECYCLED

70 billion

In 2018, Americans bought more than 70 billion plastic water bottles. Three-quarters of them ended up in landfill or an incinerator.

Container Recycling Institute, 'Bottled water', *Issues*, n.d., <container-recycling.org/index.php/issues/bottled-water>.

100%

Plastics are strong, durable, waterproof, lightweight, easy to shape and recyclable – all key properties for construction materials. All polymers are 100 per cent recyclable.

Cestari, Sibele, 'Why plastic waste is an ideal building material', *Future Planet*, BBC, 20 August 2020, <bbc.com/future/article/20200819-why-plastic-waste-is-an-ideal-building-material>.

100 billion

100 billion garments are produced globally each year. One-third of these go to landfill within the first year of purchase.

McCallion, Aleasha, 'Coming full circle on fast fashion for a sustainable future', *Lens*, 31 March 2021, <lens.monash.edu/@environment/2021/03/31/1382982/coming-full-circle-on-fast-fashion-for-a-sustainable-future>.

The breakdown and reconstitution of waste is the new frontier when it comes to recycled building materials. Although reuse should always be considered before recycling, sometimes there is no worth or value left in the material or item for reuse. When this happens, upcycling the waste material to make a new product is a good solution.

Recycling processes can also allow non-construction waste materials, such as post-consumer waste, to be transformed into construction materials. Residential projects can include these in their projects as structural materials, cladding or finishes. The projects discussed in this section use insulation made from old denim, rammed-earth bricks made from construction waste, benchtops made from old plastic chopping boards and terrazzo made from recycled glass.

More and more of these products are being developed and put into production all over the world and are ready to be picked up and used by architects, interior designers and consumers.

Left: Detail of recycled plastic used at Mountain View.
Centre: Furniture made from construction waste at Alexander House.
Right: Bathroom terrazzo made from recycled glass at Alfondac apartment.

Reuse Flat

LOCATION	London, UK
ARCHITECT	Arboreal Architecture
REUSED MATERIAL	Denim used for insulation, brick used for paving and gabion wall, timber used for wall lining, reclaimed timber for flooring and kitchen cabinets

When Tom Raymont of Arboreal Architecture was first approached by the owner of Reuse Flat, the priority was a thermal retrofit, which involves installing a new interior lining to improve the thermal performance of the flat. But even though the project began as an attempt to lower carbon emissions, it ended up being more about reuse. Existing materials were carefully removed and reused wherever possible, and any new materials that had to be brought in were selected for their recycled content or other sustainable properties.

This London flat is part of a school building that was constructed in 1910. Nearly 100 years later, the school moved across the road and the building was converted into flats. The brick walls did not have any insulation – they were simply drylined with plasterboard. Now, the flat has been redesigned for the 21st century, with a focus on thermal performance to reduce the need to burn fossil fuels. The flat was quite dark at the back, so it has been opened to the light and to create a connection with the outdoors. The design includes a large kitchen where the chef owner can cook and run cooking lessons.

Reuse was a vital aspect for both the architect and client. 'We both shared the pain of throwing things away that still had usefulness,' says Raymont. 'Even though it was originally about carbon emissions, it became reuse that we were passionate about.'

From the very beginning of the process, Raymont enlisted the contractor's help to deconstruct the existing interiors, including walls and flooring. The brick back wall was dismantled carefully, and whole bricks were used to pave the outdoor seating area. The floor was also taken up, and although it turned out to be lesser in quality expected – a little hardwood on ply rather than all hardwood, it was sawn, sanded, oiled and used as wall panels. 'We didn't know, when they started taking apart the floor, whether it would come up in useable pieces,' says Raymont. 'But even with something that was relatively low in quality, we were still able to come up with something quite useful.'

Materials that were lesser quality or had been damaged in the process of disassembly were downcycled, used to fill a gabion wall. A gabion wall is a wire-framed wall filled with miscellaneous materials that are often low in quality. In this case, broken bricks and pieces of broken concrete were used to fill most of the wall, which separates the back garden from the neighbours. Otherwise unusable timber was also added towards the top so that its eventual decay wouldn't cause the wall to subside. The timber pieces had holes drilled in them to encourage insect habitation, and the wall was planted with climbers.

'As architects, it's not about choosing the right coffee cup, it's about radically transforming the way we specify materials and design for their assembly and disassembly,' says Raymont. An estimated 20 m² of 'waste' (the equivalent of 250 bin bags) came from the deconstruction phase, but a new use was found for 43 per cent of it on site.

To achieve the desired thermal performance, insulation made from recycled denim and cotton textile waste was used. Rather than hiding this blue-grey insulation behind the walls, timber panels reclaimed from the old flooring were screwed over the top of it in such a way that the layers are visible. This also means that this design solution can be disassembled for future reuse. 'Someone asked me if we could write a guidebook, almost like disassembly instructions,' says Raymont, who believes that design for deconstruction is the future of sustainable design. 'The madness is that image of the wrecking ball coming in and destroying a building. We try not to use the word demolition, we say deconstruction.'

Reclaimed materials were also found for other parts of the new interior, including reclaimed oak for the kitchen and the kitchen sink. Old windows were moved from the back wall and reused to create a glazed partition in the office and the old granite worktop was repolished and installed as preparation surfaces in the new kitchen.

The lighting in the kitchen is another feature designed for disassembly and was intended as a visual expression of energy use. Rather than being hidden, the electrical wires for the ceiling lights are routed through stainless-steel surface-level conduits usually used in medical applications, creating an almost sculptural network of wires in snaking metal overhead. This choice was about highlighting electricity use for the inhabitants – if you can see the electricity, perhaps you will be more mindful of its use.

Reuse Flat is not just about saving energy, nor is it just about reuse. It sets a benchmark for how to design for eventual disassembly at the end of life. 'The final project can now be considered a material bank; the exposed fasteners, no glue and robust materials allow for its future deconstruction,' says Raymont. Across all these categories, Reuse Flat is outstanding. The architects estimate that 89 per cent of the materials could be directly reused elsewhere, 10 per cent could be recycled and only 1 per cent would contribute to future waste. And even the new insulation is made from recycled waste.

Right: Rear entry with views to the main living–dining space.

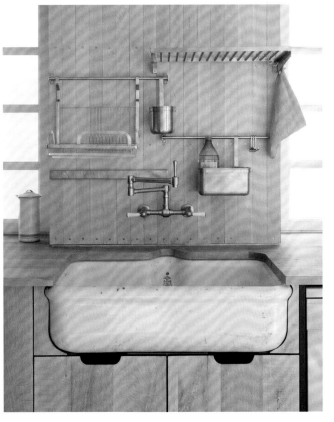

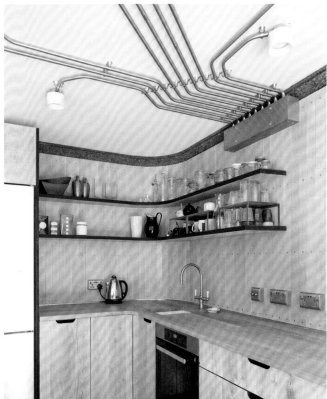

Top left: Salvaged kitchen sink.
Bottom left: Recycled denim insulation.

Top right: Reclaimed timber in the kitchen.
Bottom right: Metal conduit for lighting.

The wire-framed gabion wall is filled with brick, concrete and timber.

A new use was found for nearly half of the construction waste on site.

Recycled

The grey wall insulation is made with recycled denim
and cotton textile waste.

RECYCLED: DENIM USED FOR INSULATION

Denim is one of the most worn types of textiles and it is a big problem for waste generation. But it can also be recycled. The material used to line the interiors of Reuse Flat is called Inno-Therm in the United Kingdom (and Metisse in France). It is a low-carbon recycled acoustic and thermal natural fibre insulation material that is non-itch and non-toxic, and includes an antibacterial and fungicide treatment and a fire retardant. It has a very low embodied energy, using 70 per cent less energy to manufacture than conventional insulation, and can be recycled after use.

In the main kitchen and living space, the insulation has been installed directly onto the wall without glue. It is held in place by planks of reclaimed wood screwed over the top of it. The blue-grey insulation can be seen peeking through the planks – it was a deliberate choice to show the material at the cornice. 'In the detailing we allowed the insulation to run above and turn forming a cornice,' says Raymont. 'It has a thermal value because the corner can be a place for heat loss. It has a thermal purpose, but it also has a visual expression.'

This material proves that it's not just construction waste that can be recycled in new houses and apartments, but post-consumer waste too.

ARCHITECT	Arboreal Architecture
PROJECT TEAM	Tom Raymont
CONTRACTOR	Macek Siwon
CABINETRY	Constructive and Co
PHOTOGRAPHY	Agnese Sanvito

Above: The timber-lined walls all are backed with recycled insulation.
Right: An existing granite work surface was refinished for use.

Off-Grid House

LOCATION	Blue Mountains, Australia
ARCHITECT	Anderson Architecture
REUSED MATERIAL	Fibre-cement board

A fibre-cement board made from 60 per cent recycled content was used as both cladding and decking on architect Simon Anderson's new home in the Blue Mountains, 50 kilometres north-west of Sydney. The material was an important find for Anderson – not only is it made of recycled content, it protects the house from fires. This is an important consideration in this part of Australia, which is prone to hot summers and not-infrequent bushfires. This project was also an exercise in designing a net-zero-emissions family home that is completely off the grid.

The first step was to find the right site for the house. This plot of land is off the grid, and it also had a clearing with an approval to build obtained by the previous owners. Anderson had several stringybark trees felled at the edge of the clearing and kept on site to dry out. This timber was later milled at a local sawmill and used in the hallway and bathroom, for some of the furniture and bookshelves, and in the exposed joists. 'It sat there for six months drying out while the house was coming up and we utilised that wood in parts of the structure,' says Anderson. 'I'm pretty proud that we were able to use that timber.'

The house is simple in plan – a long rectilinear form with living areas at one end and bedrooms and bathrooms at the other, and a partial split in the building in the centre, opposite the entry. The two volumes have steeply pitched skillion roofs oriented in opposite directions. In the sleeping areas, the roof is oriented so the sun floods in during the day, and in the living areas, the roof is oriented towards full sun to make the most of solar absorption for the solar panels. This meant the main living space had less sun than might be ideal, but Anderson embraced the cave-like interiors. 'Inspiration for the design of the living area was found in the escarpments with their grey, weathered outer faces and luminescent sandstone undercrofts,' says Anderson. 'Glass doors slide away on two faces of this room, creating a cave-like cantilever and blurring the indoor–outdoor boundary with the sunlit deck beyond.'

A large deck extends the living space at one end and a smaller deck is situated outside the bedroom. The house is designed so that large shutters can come down if the owners have to evacuate due to a bushfire, while the external cladding protects the house and its contents. The house has high levels of insulation and air-tightness, with double glazing and external shading. The flooring is a black oxide insulated concrete floor with hydronic in-slab heating that uses a heat pump system. The house is low in power consumption and has solar panels with battery storage, plus a worm farm sewage system and 30,000 litre rainwater storage.

Anderson designed Off-Grid House as a family home, but also as an exercise in constructing bushfire-proof buildings that are self-sufficient in power, water and sewerage – completely off the grid. He has since worked on six or seven other houses in the Blue Mountains and other parts of rural

Above: The cladding is a fibre-cement board made from recycled content.
Right: This property in the Australian bush is totally off the grid.

New South Wales. 'It was an experiment,' he says. 'There are things on this house I wouldn't have done with a client. But when you're the client, there's a little more leeway.'

In the last couple of years, the options for green building materials have improved – now there is readily available green concrete that Anderson would have used if it had been an option. Sometimes, to be truly sustainable, you need to push the boundaries. Innovation is vital in a future where recycled materials are regularly used for construction.

Left: Bush views from the picture window above the kitchen sink.
Above: Black oxide insulated concrete floor with hydronic in-slab heating.

Glass doors slide away to open onto the deck and the
surrounding views.

The small wood fire bolsters the underfloor heating and heat
recovery system.

Built-in window seat in the bedrooms.

Recycled

Timber from the trees that had to be felled on site was used
in the bedrooms.

The deck and cladding have substantial recycled content.

RECYCLED: FIBRE-CEMENT BOARD

Off-Grid House is clad in a low-carbon fibre-cement board that gives the appearance of timber. This product, produced by Ubiq, has the highest possible rating in terms of bushfire protection, with a rating of BAL 40 and BAL FZ. 'I was a bit enamoured by the product and thought, "Why don't we use that?",' explains Anderson. 'The premise behind the cladding is that it's this protective skin – it's got this rough textural black look.'

Sustainability is an important aspect of Anderson's architectural practice, and he has seen a slow but steady uptake of sustainable ideas from over the years. 'Now, everyone wants to have a rainwater tank, solar panels and natural light but that drops off if the budget's not there,' he says. 'The thing I've noticed the most is if you start to talk about sustainable design they glaze over, but when you start talking about saving money, it's different. My wife's a scientist so we try to blend science and arts in the architecture, using modelling to show how to implement sustainable ideas.'

ARCHITECT	Anderson Architecture
BUILDER	Against the Grain Building
ENGINEER	Partridge and Bill Anderson
PHOTOGRAPHY	Nick Bowers

Above: The verandah roof folds in to keep the house protected in the event of fires.

Alexander House

LOCATION	Sydney, Australia
ARCHITECT	Alexander &CO
REUSED MATERIAL	Rammed-earth panels for feature walls and outdoor furniture; bricks made from recycled materials; reclaimed timbers for ceilings, flooring and structure

Architect Jeremy Bull of Alexander &CO worked with a manufacturer to develop a new building material made from demolition waste to use in Alexander House. The house is right next door to Bull's family home in the inner-Sydney suburb of Bondi Junction and acts as spillover space for his family as well as being a hub for the 20 or so staff employed in his architecture and interiors studio. The new material was used for three feature walls plus an outdoor furniture set. The house also features reclaimed timbers and bricks made from recycled materials.

Alexander House is a semi-residential space – a 21st century hybrid. It has space for quiet work on a laptop, business meetings and staff catch-ups, but is also great for watching a movie with the kids in the evening. During the COVID-19 lockdown, Alexander House was used more than ever as an extension of the family home, as the staff worked from home and Bull's four children took over the residence for homeschooling.

The space is dynamic – not 100 per cent residential, but a fluid space that suits contemporary life. 'We wanted to make the house feel like a hotel lobby, transient, where the lobby becomes the epicentre of life,' says Bull. 'We wanted the dynamism of the hotel lobby with a floor plan that could be futureproofed for lots of different purposes. That was the jambalaya of ideas we started with.'

The residential layout is designed to accommodate its flexible use and means the house can be converted back into a traditional home later. The front elevation is that of a traditional Victorian semi-detached house in black and white. The front door is at the side of the building and opens to a small entry hall. The floor is split so that the front quarter of the house, including the entry hall, is offset from the main floorplates. From the entry hall, you look above waist-height to the living room, or below, through a perforated screen, to the basement level below, where a large open-plan space is currently used as a workspace.

The main ground-floor space is large and open. At one end is the kitchen, featuring a large pink concrete island bench, leather banquette seating and a table, and at the other end is the living space with soft furnishings. The outdoor patio has furniture made from reclaimed waste.

Upstairs, on the mezzanine, a double-height void above the kitchen is overlooked by a balcony-style office space that has a long concrete desk. There is also a timber-clad library that Bull uses as his main office and a bathroom and shower. On the second floor is a large bedroom space that is sometimes used by visiting interstate colleagues, a table where the kids can do their homeschooling, and a living room. On this level, there is also a toilet and a steam room. Staff can use the living spaces for meetings with clients or work from their laptop at one of the many tables.

Probably the most impressive innovation in Alexander House is the rammed-earth panels, made from recycled construction materials and pressed on site. Reclaimed timbers were used in the structure and to line the first-floor ceiling and bedroom floors. The bricks that line the stairs are called Luytens bricks. They are made by the Natural Brick Co from recycled pine and concrete.

There is a great variety of materials used in the house, including those made in collaboration with artisans, like the custom pink concrete bench that had to be craned in. Other custom items include leather curtains, ceramic tableware made from recycled porcelain, light pendants, a timber banquette and library shelving. Some pieces of furniture were bought as vintage pieces, and others are family heirlooms.

Sustainability was an incredibly important part of the design of Alexander House. The house has two underground water tanks with a total capacity of 20,000 litres – this water is used for the sanitary and irrigation system. A greywater reuse system is used for the garden. Solar panels generate up to 45 kwh of power per day with a 13 kwh battery, supplying 60 to 80 per cent of the house's electrical needs, as well as all water heating. Underground worm farms process up to 30 litres of food waste every week.

Alexander House was always intended to be a showcase for materials as well as a testing ground for sustainable design – Bull calls it a 'laboratory'. 'I have eco-anxiety all the time but, for most of my luxury residential clients, it's not even a consideration,' says Bull. 'We try to Trojan horse some of this into our projects for them.' Part of the problem is what Bull calls the 'nuts and berries' aesthetic that goes with the concept of sustainable design, which doesn't appeal to everyone in the luxury category.

The opportunity that Bull and his team have seized with Alexander House is a proof of concept. It demonstrates that sustainable design and the use of innovative sustainable materials does not have to come with a 'look' but can be completely contemporary.

Right: The Victorian terrace has decorative wrought iron at the front.

The kitchen is dominated by a huge pink custom concrete
island bench.

This semi-residential workplace has a fully-functional kitchen.

Top left: Living room on the ground floor.
Bottom left: Mezzanine with reclaimed timber floor.

Top right: Marble sink in the mezzanine-level bathroom.
Bottom right: Six-metre long banquette seating.

Top left: Custom vanity in the entry-level bathroom.
Bottom left: The dining room opens to the garden.

Top right: Dining room end wall.
Bottom right: Concrete staircase landing.

The brick screened wall in the living room is made
from recycled materials.

On the stair landing, a grey-and-beige striped wall is made
of rammed earth construction waste.

Top left: Steam shower with pink tiles in the loft.
Bottom left: Custom walnut table.

Top right: The guest bedroom upstairs.
Bottom right: A seating nook in the kitchen.

Reclaimed oregon timber was used for the ceilings
in the study.

Alexander House

RECYCLED: RAMMED-EARTH PANELS

Bull worked with Will Munro and the team at Re. Studio Collective to develop a pressed earth panel made from recycled building waste. 'Will had emailed me a long time ago about this brick product,' says Bull. 'It hadn't been used before. He sent me an image of a palette of bricks in the factory and it was the perfect solve for this privacy screen we wanted in the living room.' The material was pressed on site from construction waste and stacked as a grid to create a semi-transparent screen built into the wall of the house.

Bull and Munro were keen to experiment with different waste materials and colours. 'Sustainability at its core doesn't run out – it's self-sustaining,' says Bull. 'It's showing that we can genuinely make buildings out of waste building materials.' They designed two more panels– one opposite the entry in grey and black that allows a screened view of the basement, and one near the top of the staircase with vertical stripes of grey and beige. They also developed a furniture setting for the outdoor room, adding a pink oxide to it to complement the kitchen island. Munro's studio then developed the furniture series and released it commercially.

ARCHITECT	Alexander &CO
PROJECT TEAM	Jeremy Bull, Shelby Griffiths, Harrison, Bontrager, Anson Li, Tess Glasson, Sam Jones
BUILDER	Fairweather Constructions
STYLIST	Claire Delmar
PHOTOGRAPHY	Anson Smart

Above: Outdoor furniture made from waste was developed for the project.
Right: Rammed earth bricks made from construction waste in dark grey screen the level below.

Mo-tel House

LOCATION	London, UK
ARCHITECT	Office S&M
REUSED MATERIAL	Plastic used for bathroom countertops, marble terrazzo used for kitchen benchtops, brick grog used for light pendants

Above: Colour is used to counter the grey skies of London.
Right: The playful custom furniture unit acts as storage and seating.

When designing Mo-tel House in London's Islington, architect Catrina Stewart from Office S&M used new products made from recycled waste to convert a dark and dated Victorian townhouse into a bright and thoroughly contemporary family home. A material made from recycled post-consumer plastics was chosen for the bathroom countertops – a move that was important to the owner, whose business is about reducing fashion waste. The design of Mo-tel House focused on creating a bright, new open-plan kitchen–dining room on the lower-ground floor, plus a bathroom and staircase, and another bathroom on the ground level.

On the lower-ground floor, the rooms were so dark and damp that they couldn't be used much. Removing a wall that separated the kitchen from a storage area opened the space up, and colour, along with good lighting and mirrors, was used to bring life to the spaces. 'We were never going to be able to install big windows and so the light was always going to be a bit limited,' explains Stewart. 'We wanted to open it up and bring more character to a space that was quite simple before. The way we did that was to use different tones and shades of colour.'

Colour was used to create a sense of escape from the grey skies of London, hence the name of the project, Mo-tel. Early studies by Office S&M show a collection of colourful 3D geometric shapes, like pastel building blocks, in various shades of pink and green, as well as blue, red, yellow and navy. Some of these shapes made it to the final design and others served as general colour inspiration.

The final design for the kitchen features floor-to-ceiling sky-blue cabinets that have a curved semicircle jutting out over the top, teal-green kitchen cabinets, mint-green walls, pink tiles, a dark-green terrazzo benchtop and a dark-blue door. Block colours can also be found in the details, such as a yellow door handle, an electric-blue radiator and yellow light switches. Finding these details is a little more work than the usual, admits Stewart, but the effect is worth the effort.

In the adjoining dining space, the mint-green walls continue, and a built-in seating and storage element features two pitched steeples in pink at the top, a dark-blue backing and seat, and pink cupboards at the base, in the seat of its bench.

This multipurpose furniture brings a colourful building-block aesthetic to the design, but it is also about reducing material use. The architects have thought carefully about the family's requirements and designed one piece of furniture to meet many needs. 'If we were to build five different pieces of furniture, that would be quite wasteful,' says Stewart. 'We realised it would be better to build one piece of furniture with multiple functions that could also last longer and reduce waste.' Thoughtful features include low storage for toys and other child-safe items and wine storage that is above head height.

There are other colourful elements here – the table is mint green and the glass doors have a yellow frame. Both new bathrooms are also filled with colour. The lower-ground bathroom has black floor tiles, teal wall tiles and a pink wall, and the ground-floor bathroom has white tiles with yellow grout. 'We wanted it to be fresh and warm. And there was this idea of trying to manipulate the weather, to counteract the grey London skies.'

The use of recycled materials was encouraged by the client, who owns a fashion business that rents out clothes to reduce fashion waste and was interested in reducing waste in the house as much as possible. In the kitchen, forest-green terrazzo made from marble chips was used. In the bathroom, the black-and-white countertops are made from old plastic chopping boards and milk bottle tops to create a marble look. The lights above the dining table are made from recycled brick grog.

'It's hugely important that we reverse what we've done in the last 200 years,' says Stewart. 'If not, we won't last long on this planet. I think it's about doing everything we can to reduce waste.' Mo-tel House combines fresh and contemporary colours with a sustainable approach to materials selection – the best of both worlds.

The kitchen has a large, pale-blue storage piece, mint stripe
near the ceiling and pink splashback.

The basement kitchen and dining room is packed
with colourful details.

Top left: A fabulous staircase.
Bottom left: Even the tableware matches.

Top right: Bathroom in pink, teal and black.
Bottom right: Kitchen detail with yellow jug.

Colourful view from the bathroom.

RECYCLED: PLASTIC COUNTERTOPS

Office S&M takes an experimental approach to architecture that extends to the use of new and emerging materials. 'We had a list of manufacturers we were really interested in working with,' says Stewart. 'It just takes a bit more time to find these pieces, but as a practice, it's something we're interested in.'

The bathroom countertops are made from recycled plastic in mottled black and white – almost like the colouring of oyster shells. The product contains plastics from old chopping boards and packaging. It comes from a microfactory called Smile Plastics that transforms waste plastics into useable interior finishes.

Reusing waste is important for Stewart. 'I grew up in a consumerist society where things were often used once and thrown away,' she says. 'We're still in that place. Often supermarkets try to shield people from where these products have come from and how they've been made. It's really important to educate yourself about how things are made and how wasteful these processes are.'

ARCHITECT	Office S&M
PROJECT TEAM	Catrina Stewart, Hugh McEwen
ENGINEER	Foster Structures
CONTRACTOR AND FURNITURE BUILD	McElligott Building
PHOTOGRAPHY	French + Tye

Above: Recycled plastic surfaces in black and white grace the bathroom countertops.
Right: Stunning geometries and colours.

Mountain View

LOCATION	London, UK
ARCHITECT	CAN
REUSED MATERIAL	Plastic for kitchen benchtops and cabinets, decorative plaster mouldings in living room, reclaimed bricks, recycled aluminium

Mat Barnes, the director of architecture and design studio CAN, embraces creativity, including myriad unexpected sources of inspiration, bold colours and new materials, including those made from recycled waste. In the transformation of his South London home, Barnes has created a design full of surprises and invention.

The semi-detached Edwardian house was in a bad state when Barnes and his family first moved in. He remembers shutting the front door one evening and the ceiling plaster in the entry hallway collapsing behind him. But, despite the state of the property, it had good bones.

The biggest changes have been made to the ground floor. The living room at the front of the house was retained, although it looks completely different, and a collection of smaller rooms towards the back has been transformed into a long dining space that flows into another living room, part of the new extension at the back of the house. The floor of the open-plan kitchen, dining and living room has been lowered, bringing the rooms more in line with the outdoor spaces and creating generous ceilings. Glazing brings in natural light.

Material use in the house is inventive. The 'mountain' in the name of the house comes from the exterior of the back elevation, which has a roofline finished in a lightweight material created by passing bubbles through molten aluminium as it cures. Barnes was inspired by an image of Disneyland's Matterhorn Mountain under construction, with spindly metal pipes holding up a fake mountain peak.

Here, the 'mountain' is used as a finish for the roof, but also gives a surreal impression of something heavy being supported by a series of light, red-and-white metal poles. 'We needed to finish the edge in something, and we thought, "How can we make the roof [look] as heavy as possible?" and a mountain is the heaviest thing,' says Barnes. 'It's made of 100 per cent recycled aluminium and it's so light that one person could lift the whole thing. It's a great time for new materials.'

Another new material has been used for the kitchen cabinets and benchtops – a marble-look product that Barnes has used in alternating blue and black that is made of recycled plastic chopping boards and bottle tops. Elsewhere, Barnes again took inspiration from outside the architecture profession. Between the kitchen and the living room towards the back of the house, the partially demolished brick wall was inspired by the crumbling brick walls in the movie *Trainspotting*. The bricks taken down were relaid elsewhere in the project, and the remaining wall was painted and left as is.

Barnes says that, as the client, he could decide to leave some elements alone. 'Because I'm an architect, I'm interested in seeing the structure of the building,' he explains. 'Plus, if you can use the structure as the finish as well, you're getting more bang for your buck.'

In the living room, another unexpected waste material has been used to great effect. Fragments of decorative mouldings have been attached to the walls and painted cobalt blue, along with the walls, ceiling and floor, with a sofa and rug to match. The idea was to create a cosy living room for winter – a room that is the complete opposite to the rest of the ground floor. 'I like designing buildings with lots of different rooms. In the winter you want cosy and dimly lit,' says Barnes.

At the time, Barnes was doing an exhibition at the John Soane Museum and was inspired by the way Soane's architectural elements were arranged together on one wall. Barnes asked a local plastermaker if they had any seconds or broken parts. They had a lot. 'He said, "Everything on the shelves you can see, you can take – I've been meaning to do a clear-out." It ties into the reuse – stuff that was otherwise destined for the bin.'

As well as being full of inventive ideas, Mountain View is also remarkable for its use of colour. As well as the blue in the living room, there are metal beams and trusses painted in bright red in one room and blue in another. The underside of the stairs is painted marigold yellow, and there is a grey-and-white checkerboard pattern in the living space.

'In modernism there's almost a fear of colour, that it shows too much emotion. Then there's this whole thing that the colours need to match,' says Barnes. 'To me it's totally arbitrary. One person says colours match and another person says they don't match. The way we approached it in the house was we just picked the right colour for that wall. Then we thought of a colour for the stairs that would be nice for that element. We developed it on site.'

This house is not shy about its green credentials: 'WASTE NOT, WANT NOT' is spelled out in black-and-white tiles in the stair treads between the entry hall and the kitchen. The motto is inspired by the same words on an Edwardian plate that is now on display on the mantlepiece. For Barnes, the phrase being visible from the kitchen is a reminder to the family not to waste food as well as being about construction waste.

Upstairs, he added an extra bedroom and bathroom to the floor plan. The design fades gradually from the vibrancy of the communal ground-floor spaces to the quiet neutral of the bedrooms, with a pastel mint-green staircase helping with the transition. The only bright room on the upper floors is a blue-and-white check tiled bathroom – inspired by blue tiles found in one of the old fireplaces – with burnt-orange ceilings.

Mountain View is a house full of ideas. The best of these come from the prioritisation of materials made from reclaimed materials, as well as a general attitude about reducing waste in construction.

Right: View from the back extension to the new kitchen and dining room.

Blue living room with scraps of decorative plaster waste.

Mint-green balustrade.

Bold bathroom in blue, white and burnt orange.

Top left: 'Waste not, want not' plate.
Bottom left: A sculpture of red arrows by Liam Fallon.

Top right: Grey-and-white tiles in the second living space.
Bottom right: Mint-green and orange stairs.

Vibrant kitchen with alternating blue and grey recycled plastic
benches made from old plastic chopping boards and bottle tops.

Roughcast render walls in the dining room.

Top left: The 'mountain' through the skylight.
Bottom left: Second living room.

Top right: These tiles were made to look like survey targets.
Bottom right: Aluminium 'mountain'.

The design makes a feature of 'crumbling' brick walls.

Recycled

RECYCLED: PLASTIC FOR KITCHEN BENCHTOPS AND CABINETS

The kitchen cabinets, benchtops and island are all clad in a marble-look material made by Smile Plastics from recycled plastic chopping boards and bottle tops. Barnes used two different colours from their Classics range – black and white, and blue and white – in alternating cabinets, and the black-and-white material covers the entire benchtop.

Barnes had wanted to use these products for a while. 'I really like the idea that when you're chopping on your chopping board kitchen worktop, thousands of people have been chopping on these chopping boards already,' he says. 'It's this romantic idea of it being used for the same thing but in a different way.'

For Barnes, finding new materials that haven't been used before, or maybe not in an architectural context, is also exciting. 'Fundamentally, I like trying different things because if you do the same thing over and over again, it's quite boring.'

ARCHITECT	CAN
PROJECT TEAM	Mat Barnes
STRUCTURAL ENGINEER	Hardman Structural Engineers
MAIN CONTRACTOR	Catalin London Ltd
KITCHEN MAKER	Harry Lawson
PHOTOGRAPHY	Jim Stephenson

Above: The kitchen benches made from recycled post-consumer content creates a distinctive new look.

Alfondac

LOCATION	Reus, Spain
ARCHITECT	Axiopluc
REUSED MATERIAL	Terrazzo

Recycled terrazzo and locally sourced plywood are the two key materials that make up the new interiors of Alfondac, an apartment in the Catalonian city of Reus, Spain designed by architect David Tapias of Axiopluc. This simple material palette belies the complexity of this project, which is not only an exercise in upcycling a derelict apartment, but also a radical architectural intervention activated through a modular kit-of-parts called the Homeful system.

The Homeful system was created to solve a common problem – home owners who have enough money to buy an apartment, but not enough to pay for a new interior. Rents are cheap in Spain and, as a result, old apartments lie empty and unused. 'It is often too costly and tiring to undertake a reform, with high levels of uncertainty about time, costs and outcome,' says Tapias. 'This leads to extremely low-quality renovations to maximise sales or rental profits, or expensive refurbishment for the privileged few.'

Alfondac allowed the architects to show how one such apartment, empty for two years, could be completely renovated using an affordable modular kit. The resulting apartment is a guesthouse and a living laboratory where visitors can test and give feedback on the system. The name 'Alfondac' is derived from the Arabic word *al-fondaq* – a place for an overnight stay for travellers and traders as well as a community warehouse for surplus grain. 'The name is a tribute to the Muslim heritage of our territory of the Camp de Tarragona,' says Tapias.

The first step to making the Homeful system affordable was to use as much of the existing building fabric as possible, without adding expensive interior finishes. For Alfondac, that meant repairing the existing tiled flooring that was found when the old floor was removed. Concrete was used to fill gaps in the tiling and polished to create a perfectly serviceable floor that also contains the history of its past use. 'Normally you would take it out, but we decided to keep it, not creating more waste than necessary,' says Tapias. 'In fact, the quality is probably much better than any new material you can apply.'

Problems with the structure were also handled creatively. Wooden beams that had been bent out of shape over the years had to be made more structurally sound. Rather than replacing them or adding heavy steel beams, the architects went for a more minimal approach – a series of lightweight steel cables that support the weight of the ceiling.

Other choices were made to keep material use to a minimum, while adding the necessary elements to insulate the apartment. When the ceiling the last owner had put up was removed, the walls and ceiling were left unfinished, showing the scars from the previous architecture.

Walls are raw brick, painted white, and the architects also put in new plywood windows and insulated the thinner existing walls to retain heat in winter. Heating is provided by a pellet stove.

The interior design is also totally radical. Rather than planning a series of rooms – kitchen, living, bedroom, bathroom – the Homeful system places the main elements near where the water and electricity are already located, saving the cost of moving these services. In this apartment, that meant that the kitchen and bathroom were placed side by side.

Rather than creating custom bathroom and kitchen cabinets, the kitchen and bathroom are made up of several modular elements that are standard across the Homeful system. Most of these modular furniture items are made of just two materials – terrazzo made with hand-picked recycled glass and timber plywood grown in northern Spain. They are also regular and square – the terrazzo shower floor, the bathroom laundry sink, the kitchen bench with induction cooktop, and the kitchen bench with two holes for garbage disposal are all 1 metre by 1 metre.

Around these modular elements are plywood doors, folding tabletops, plus shelving and chairs. This creates options to close off the bathroom, move the kitchen to a long bench-style or put everything away when more space is needed. The kitchen bench is on wheels to make this transformation easier.

Another transformable plywood structure in the middle of the apartment looks like a miniature house. This is Shelterhood – a bed that turns into a dining table during the day. Shelterhood came from an earlier experimental project that encouraged children to make a tiny house. A series of different cubbyhouses were made as part of that project – some of which could be assembled by children and some that were a little more complicated. This tiny plywood house is only as wide and long as a double bed and features walls and a pitched roof.

Part of this experiment was about how little the architects could intervene in the space to make it habitable. The modular system can also be easily removed and reused in another space: 'Design for disassembly is a natural approach,' says Tapias. 'Hopefully it can last in that place for many years, but if it needs to change, the materials can be taken from that place.'

Sustainable material use is also a vital part of Alfondac. The terrazzo was made with recycled glass chosen by the architect, and the plywood was sourced from Navarra in the north of Spain after extensive research into the most environmentally friendly options for timber.

Although not currently occupied full-time as a residential apartment, Alfondac is an experimental space that aims to bring a residential design back to bare bones. The apartment embraces its history and a totally new approach to design. What is really needed to make a building into a home? Who said a kitchen should be long and thin? And why shouldn't we sleep in a mobile bedroom whose walls are only as wide as the bed itself?

Importantly, this project also shows how to minimise waste in an affordable apartment redesign and how to select materials that have minimum impact on the environment and can be used again and again.

Right: Terrazzo basins and benches are made from recycled glass.

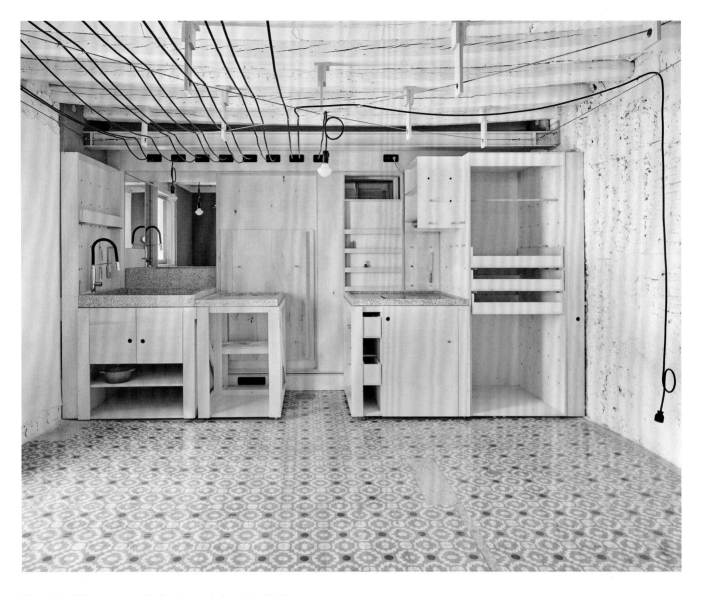

The original tiles were repaired and resealed, and the kitchen packs away completely.

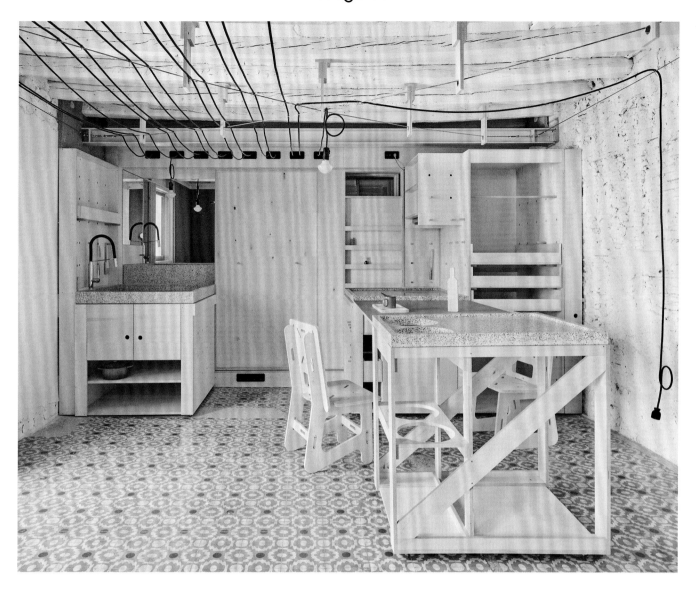

The modular pieces can be brought out to form a fully
functioning kitchen.

Left: Shelterhood is a plywood structure that can be used as a bed.
Above: The same structure also transforms into a dining room.

RECYCLED: TERRAZZO

Five large pieces of terrazzo were used to create the modular Homeful system, including shower, sinks and benches. The terrazzo was made by Huguet Mallorca from pieces of broken green and brown glass, selected by the architect, and bonded with fully recycled cement. Huguet Mallorca's green label cement generates 35 per cent less emissions than standard cements, and the terrazzo is thinner than those in the past, reducing the amount of raw material and transport required. 'Whatever we build needs to last as long as possible, creating the least waste as possible, resourced from renewable materials,' says Tapias. 'It's not easy to turn a destructive industry like construction into one that has a positive impact on the environment. That's a total change of paradigm. And we need to change fast.'

ARCHITECT	Axiopluc
PROJECT TEAM	David Tapias, Ricard Pau
CARPENTER	Rels
PHOTOGRAPHY	José Hevia

Above: View from the bathroom to the kitchen.

Following pages, Left: The dining room at Alexander House opens to the outdoors.
Right (inset): Profile of Casey House with grey exterior.
Right (border): Garden with recycled waste furniture pieces at Alexander House.

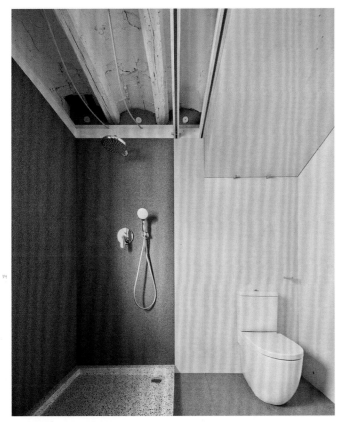

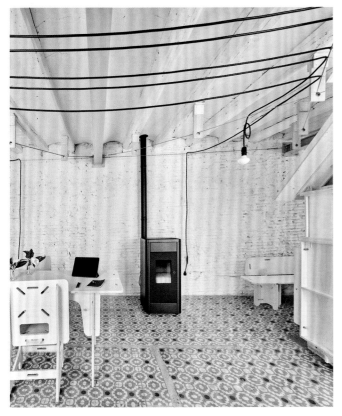

Top left: The bathroom with terrazzo shower base.
Bottom left: A pellet stove provides warmth.

Top right: A cable system offers structural support.
Bottom right: Detail of the plywood dining space.

RESOURCES

Resources

MATERIALS MADE FROM WASTE

The research and development of construction materials made from reconstituted waste is undergoing huge growth. Whether it's construction waste or post-consumer waste, these second-life materials are being upcycled into structural materials, cladding and interior finishes all over the world. Here is a small selection.

1 FIRECLAY TILES

HEADQUARTERS: USA
MATERIAL: Tiles, glass and brick made from recycled materials
WEBSITE: fireclaytile.com
Fireclay Tiles sells tiles, glass and brick. Eighty per cent of their products are made from recycled materials, including granite fines, a waste material produced when cutting granite. This image is from a collaboration with Block Shop.

2 FORESSO

HEADQUARTERS: UK
MATERIAL: Timber terrazzo made from wood including offcuts and waste
WEBSITE: foresso.co.uk
Foresso sells a tiled finish for walls, floors and benches that is made with 65 per cent wood content, including timber offcuts, planing waste and wood dust.

3 HONEXT

HEADQUARTERS: Spain
MATERIAL: Interior panels made from cellulose waste
WEBSITE: honextmaterial.com
Honext sells recyclable non-toxic panels that can be cut, drilled and sanded like wood, but are made of 100 per cent paper waste.

4 HUGUET MALLORCA

HEADQUARTERS: Spain
MATERIAL: Terrazzo made from recycled glass
WEBSITE: huguetmallorca.com
Huguet Mallorca sells terrazzo, tiles, basins and benchtops made from 100 per cent recycled cement and aggregates, including glass. See Alfondac (pages 256–263).

5 INNO-THERM

HEADQUARTERS: UK
MATERIAL: Insulation made from recycled denim
WEBSITE: inno-therm.com
Inno-Therm (called Metisse in France) is an insulation material made from 85 per cent recycled denim and cotton. See Reuse Flat (pages 206–213).

6 NATURE SQUARED

HEADQUARTERS: Switzerland
MATERIAL: Tiles made from eggshells
WEBSITE: naturesquared.com
Nature Squared sells tiles including the CArrelé Collection designed by Elaine Yan Ling Ng, which is made with eggshells.

7 PAPERTILE
HEADQUARTERS: Canada
MATERIAL: Wall tiles made from recycled paper
WEBSITE: papertile.ca
Papertile sells wall tiles with acoustic properties designed by Dear Human and made from 100 per cent post-consumer recycled paper.

8 PRETTY PLASTIC
HEADQUARTERS: Netherlands
MATERIAL: Cladding material made from upcycled PVC
WEBSITE: prettyplastic.nl
Pretty Plastic sells tile cladding made from household plastic waste including old window frames, downspouts and rain gutters.

9 RE. STUDIO COLLECTIVE
HEADQUARTERS: Australia
MATERIAL: Panels and furniture made from recycled construction waste
INSTAGRAM: re.studio_collective
Re. Studio Collective sells a pressed earth panel and furniture series made from recycled building waste. See Alexander House (pages 224–235).

10 REALLY
HEADQUARTERS: Denmark
MATERIAL: Board and felt made from recycled textiles
WEBSITE: kvadrat.dk
Owned by Kvadrat, Really sells textile board, melamine and acoustic felt made from end-of-life cotton and wool sourced from textile industries, industrial laundries and Kvadrat cut-offs.

11 SMILE PLASTICS
HEADQUARTERS: UK
MATERIAL: Benchtops made from old chopping boards and milk bottle lids
WEBSITE: smile-plastics.com
Smile Plastics sells panels made from recycled waste, including the Classics Collection which is made from 100 per cent recycled plastic. See Mo-tel House (pages 236–243) and Mountain View (pages 244–255).

12 UBIQ
HEADQUARTERS: Australia
MATERIAL: Decking and cladding made from recycled content
WEBSITE: ubiq.com.au
Ubiq sells a fibre-cement board made from 60 per cent recycled content. See Off-Grid House (pages 214–223).

ARCHITECTURE AND INTERIOR DESIGN STUDIOS

All houses and apartments selected for this book include at least one reclaimed or recycled material, and many include more than one. All the projects were designed by architects or interior designers and have fully finished interiors as well as exteriors. These homes are in Europe, North America, Oceania and Asia.

Above, left to right: Entry to Casey House (page 166); Reclaimed pine flooring in Casey House; Marble staircase in Alexander House (page 244); Living room of the old house at Ruang Tekuni (page 104).

ADJAYE ASSOCIATES: adjaye.com

ALEXANDER &CO: alexanderand.co

ANDERSON ARCHITECTURE: andersonarchitecture.com.au

ANDREW FRANZ ARCHITECT: andrewfranz.com

ANN EDGERTON: annedgerton.com

ARBOREAL ARCHITECTURE: arborealarchitecture.com

AXIOPLUC: axiopluc.net

BREATHE: breathe.com.au

CAMILLE HERMAND ARCHITECTURES: camillearchitectures.com

CAMPOS STUDIO: campos.studio

CAN: can-site.co.uk

CUMULOLIMBO STUDIO: cumulolimbo.com

DDAP ARCHITECT: ddaparchitect.com

EDITION OFFICE: edition-office.com

KADERSTUDIO: kaderstudio.eu

MARTIN SKOČEK: martinskocek.sk

MATT ELKAN ARCHITECT: mattelkanarchitect.com.au

OFFICE S&M: officesandm.com

RETROUVIUS: retrouvius.com

SIDE ANGLE SIDE: sideangleside.co

SILAA ARCHITECTS: facebook.com/silaaarchitects

STUDIO 30 ARCHITECTS: studio30architects.co.uk

STUDIO BRIGHT: studiobright.com.au

STUDIO SARANSH: studiosaransh.com

UPSTRS_: www.upstrs.co/

Reclaimed

PHOTOGRAPHERS

Agnese Sanvito: agnesesanvito.com
Albert Vecerka, Esto: esto.com/vecerka
Anson Smart: ansonsmart.com
Ben Hosking: benhosking.com.au
Casey Dunn: caseydunn.net
Clinton Weaver: clinton-weaver.com
Ed Reeve: editphoto.net
Ema Peter: emapeter.com
French + Tye: frenchandtye.com
Hervé Goluza: instagram.com/herve_goluza
Hoang Le: hoang814.tumblr.com
Ishita Sitwala, The Fishy Project: thefishyproject.com
Javier de Paz García: estudioballoon.es
Jim Stephenson: clickclickjim.com
José Hevia: josehevia.es
Matej Hakar: matejhakar.com
Nick Bowers: nickbowers.com
Rory Gardiner: rory-gardiner.com
Sonny Sandjaya: sonnysandjaya.com
Theodore Tennant: theodoretennant.com
Tom Ross: tomross.xyz
Wong Weiliang: 328productions.com.sg

FURTHER READING

Baker-Brown, Duncan, *The Re-Use Atlas: A Designer's Guide Towards the Circular Economy*, Routledge, 2017.

Devlieger, Lionel, Maarten Gielen & Rotor curatorial team (eds), *Behind the Green Door*, Oslo Architecture Triennale, 2014.

Gorgolewski, Mark, *Resource Salvation: The Architecture of Reuse*, Wiley Blackwell, 2017.

Hebel, Dirk E, Marta H Wisniewska & Felix Heisel, *Building from Waste: Recovered Materials in Architecture and Construction*, Walter de Gruyter GmbH, 2014.

McDonough, William & Michael Braungart, *The Upcycle: Beyond Sustainability – Designing for Abundance*, North Point Press, 2013.

McDonough, William and & Michael Braungart, *Cradle to Cradle: Remaking the Way We Make Things*, North Point Press, 2002.

O'Donnell, Caroline & Dillon Pranger (eds), *The Architecture of Waste: Design for a Circular Economy,* Routledge, 2021.

Space Caviar (ed.), *Non-Extractive Architecture: On Designing Without Depletion*, MIT Press, 2021.

Stockhammer, Daniel (ed.), *Upcycling: Reuse and Repurposing as a Design Principle in Architecture*, Triest Verlag, 2020.

Resources

ARTWORK CREDITS

10, 64: *Votive*, 2018, Adam Lee, Courtesy Station Gallery

12–13, 60, 66 (top left): *She will be revealed tonight,* 2020, Kirsty Budge, Courtesy Diane Singer Gallery

17: Landscape painting, by Georgia Thorpe

19: Two sculptures by Kirsten Perry

20 (top left): *Antipodean Skyscape*, 2018, Julia Silvester

20 (bottom left): Owner supplied framed artwork by their child

31: *Imperfection in space*, unknown artist

52: Artworks left to right, *Susan, Karen and Stewart*, 1995, Ray Webster; *Untitled (Tim's Early Painting)*, 1982, Tim Noble

54: Artworks left to right, *Dad & Mum (Mugshots)*, 1975, Sue Webster; *Double Negative*, 2009, Tim Noble and Sue Webster

55: White marble bust by Martinelli Antal

59, 69: *Shake Down*, 2019, Matt Arbuckle, Courtesy Diane Singer Gallery

66 (bottom right): Artworks left to right: Framed vintage Japanese, screen print stencil, Courtesy Edition Office; Framed page from vintage Ikebana book, Courtesy Edition Office

67: Framed vintage Japanese screen print stencil, Courtesy Edition Office

68: *The Kingdom*, 2020, Grant Nimmo, Courtesy Diane Singer Gallery

75: White marble bust by Martinelli Antal

79: *Eco hlava*, date unknown, Jana Farmanova

119, 122: Illustrations, Malay Doshi

128: *Sueños*, 1975, José Antonio Matesanz

132: *Modulo 14*, 1970, José Luis Matesanz

140: *Untitled*, 1973, Birdie Lusch

145: Architecture sketches by client's father

146: Artworks left to right, Photograph by Jemima Burrill; Virgin and child study by Henry Moore; Nude study by Charlotte Steel

147: Various maps, posters and rubbings, and paintings by unknown artists

150: Photograph by Jemima Burrell

160 (bottom left): Photograph by Antoine d'Agata

163, this page, above right: Artworks left to right, Photographs by Pentti Sammallahti, Michael Ackerman and Antoine d'Agata

171: Custom wall hanging by Hallie Brewer

172 : *Untitled*, 2016, Gregory Halpern

178: Artworks left to right, Charcoal drawing, 18th or 19th century Artist unknown; Portrait of a Child, 19th century, Henry W Page; Painting on wall by Wye Nergard; Painting on floor by George Speak

179: Name unknown, Percy Green, 1898

182, this page, above left: Portrait of Adam's great-grandmother

184: Quinces, date unknown, George Speake

221: Landscape painting by Natasha Daniloff

228 (top left): *Wolfhound Interior*, 2020, Justin Williams

228 (bottom right) and 234 (bottom right): *V9 Reimagining*, 2020, Greg Wood

229 (top right): *Woman with drawing*, 2019, McLean Edwards

232 (bottom right): *V9 Reimagining*, 2020, Greg Wood

245: *Vector Drift*, 2020, Glitch Textiles

247: *Untitled*, 2017, Hetty Douglas

251 (bottom left): *Aftermath*, 2019, Liam Fallon

268 (right): *Watching for the Signal*, Nez Perce, 1910, Edward S. Curtis

ACKNOWLEDGEMENTS

Thank you to Paulina de Laveaux, Rachel Carter and the team from Thames & Hudson for all your hard work, and to Lorna Hendry for your excellent edits. Thank you to Claire Orrell, who designed this book beautifully, and to the architects, interior designers and photographers who gave us permission to publish their fantastic work. Also, to my family and friends, I am so grateful for your ongoing support. And finally, a huge thank you to Chris for being wonderful, always.

Left to right: The main bedroom at Rooftop Home (page 174); Artwork in the living room at Montmorency (page 156); Two-tone bathroom at Rylett House; Upstairs landing at Rylatt House (page 142).

ABOUT THE AUTHOR

Penny Craswell is a Sydney-based editor, writer and curator who specialises in design, craft, architecture and interiors. She is the former Editor of *Artichoke* magazine, Deputy Editor of *Indesign* magazine and Creative Strategy Associate at the Australian Design Centre, and has been published widely in design periodicals, books and online media around the world. She also writes a blog called The Design Writer.

Penny's first book, *Design Lives Here: Australian interiors, furniture and lighting*, was published by Thames & Hudson in 2020.

First published in Australia in 2022
by Thames & Hudson Australia Pty Ltd
11 Central Boulevard, Portside Business Park
Port Melbourne, Naarm, Victoria 3207
ABN: 72 004 751 964

First published in the United Kingdom in 2023
By Thames & Hudson Ltd
181a High Holborn
London WC1V 7QX

First published in the United States of America in 2023
By Thames & Hudson Inc.
500 Fifth Avenue
New York, New York 10110

Thames & Hudson Australia wishes to acknowledge that Aboriginal
and Torres Strait Islander people are the first storytellers of this nation
and the traditional custodians of the land on which we live and work.
We acknowledge their continuing culture and pay respect to Elders
past, present and future.

ISBN 978-1-76076-117-2
ISBN 978-1-76076-314-5 (U.S. edition)

 A catalogue record for this
book is available from the
National Library of Australia

British Library Cataloguing-in-Publication Data
A catalogue record for this book is available from the British Library

Library of Congress Control Number 2022934867

Every effort has been made to trace accurate ownership of
copyrighted text and visual materials used in this book. Errors
or omissions will be corrected in subsequent editions, provided
notification is sent to the publisher.

Front cover:
Kyneton House by Edition Office
Photographed by Ben Hosking

Back cover:
Mountain View by CAN
Photographed by Jim Stephenson

Design: Claire Orrell
Editing: Lorna Hendry
Printed and bound in China by C&C Offset Printing Co., Ltd

FSC® is dedicated to the promotion of responsible forest management
worldwide. This book is made of material from FSC®-certified forests
and other controlled sources.

Be the first to know about our new releases, exclusive content
and author events by visiting
thamesandhudson.com.au
thamesandhudson.com
thamesandhudsonusa.com